Whispers In the Walls

Ghosts of the Rock Island Roadhouse

© 2024 by Scott Bowser

All rights reserved. No part of this book may be reproduced, stored in a retrieval system or transmitted in any form or by any form or by any means without prior written permission by the author.

To Lisa Vinar:

I would like to extend my deepest gratitude to Lisa Vinar, whose passion and dedication to preserving the history and mystery of the Rock Island Roadhouse made this book possible. Lisa, your unwavering support, insight, and enthusiasm have been the driving force behind this project. Your commitment to sharing the unique and fascinating stories of the Roadhouse has not only inspired me but has also breathed life into these pages.

Thank you for trusting me with the privilege of telling the tale of the Rock Island Roadhouse. Your love for this remarkable place is evident in every detail, and it has been an honor to collaborate with you on this journey. This book is a testament to your hard work and your belief in the importance of keeping legends alive.

Here's too many more stories to be told and mysteries to be uncovered. Thank you, Lisa, for making this book a reality.

To Kandi Slater:

I owe a tremendous debt of gratitude to Kandi Slater, whose tireless efforts and constant communication were invaluable in bringing this book to life. Kandi, your dedication in providing information, feedback, and support through countless emails and instant messages has been nothing short of remarkable. Your keen eye for detail and your commitment to this project have made a world of difference.

Thank you for always being there, whether it was to answer a quick question or to dive deep into discussions that shaped the narrative. Your contributions have been integral to the creation of this book, and I am profoundly grateful for your unwavering support and friendship.

This book is as much yours as it is mine, and I couldn't have done it without you. Thank you, Kandi, for your partnership, your hard work, and your belief in this project.

Acknowledgments

First and foremost, I would like to extend my deepest gratitude to all the individuals who took the time to share their personal paranormal experiences with me. Your courage in recounting these often intimate and chilling encounters has been the cornerstone of this book. Without your stories, this collection would not have been possible. Your willingness to open up and describe the unexplainable has not only enriched this work but has also contributed to the broader understanding of the mysterious world that surrounds us.

To each of you who reached out—whether through emails or Instant Message—I thank you. Your contributions have brought these pages to life, and I am honored to have been entrusted with your stories. It is through your shared experiences that we can continue to explore the unknown, challenge our perceptions, and keep the spirit of curiosity alive.

This book is as much yours as it is mine. Thank you for making it possible.

Table of Contents

Preface..7

The Story of the Rock Island Roadhouse by Lisa Vinar
....9

Chapter 1
    The Mob and Rock Island, Illinois.........................13

Chapter 2
    History of the Old Rock Island Roadhouse............18

Chapter 3
    The Looney Riots of 1912..24

Chapter 4
    John Looney 30

Chapter 5
    The Spirits of the Rock Island Roadhouse............38

Chapter 6
    Stories from Paranormal Investigators................49

Chapter 7
    Photo Gallery...157

Preface

The Old Rock Island Illinois Roadhouse is steeped in history and enigma, making it a captivating subject for both historians and paranormal enthusiasts. Built in 1845 by John T. Harris, the Roadhouse began as a bustling stagecoach stop on a major trade route, offering weary travelers a place to rest and refresh. Its robust timber and stone construction housed a lively common room where news and stories flowed as freely as the ale. Over time, the establishment grew to include more rooms, a larger dining area, and stables, cementing its role as a central hub of activity and commerce in Rock Island. The Prohibition era added a layer of intrigue as the Roadhouse transformed into a notorious speakeasy, complete with secret rooms and hidden passages. This colorful past set the stage for the legends and ghost stories that would later envelop the site.

Today, the Old Rock Island Illinois Roadhouse is renowned not just for its historical significance but also for its purported hauntings. Visitors and staff alike have reported a range of paranormal activities, from mysterious noises and sudden cold spots to full-bodied apparitions. The most infamous of these is the Hat Man, a shadowy figure often seen wearing a wide-brimmed hat, who is said to roam the halls and rooms of the old building. His presence, along with other spectral sightings, has turned the Roadhouse into a magnet for ghost hunters and thrill-seekers. As a preserved historical landmark, it offers a unique blend of historical education and spine-chilling encounters, ensuring that the stories and mysteries of this storied location continue to captivate and haunt all who visit.

The Story of The Rock Island Roadhouse

By Lisa Vinar

How the Haunted Rock Island Roadhouse came to be.

My husband and I purchased the property in July of 1994, it was in very poor condition.

The skylight had fallen into the pool, the upper floors were open to birds, and were covered with 2 inches of guano. As for the main floor, all the windows had been destroyed by U-Haul when they operated the building as a storage facility, it was dark with almost no lighting and there were only 2 isles down the center. The rest of them were covered from floor to ceiling with storage units, most of the gym floor was rotting due to water damage.

This was our start. With my husband's vision and both of our hard work you can see what we accomplished.

My husband Dan passed away in 2013, so my mother who lived a block down the street would come almost every day to answer the phone or help where she could.

Unfortunately, she passed away in 2016, this is when the spirits let me know they were here with us.

The first occurrence is when two of my boys were working on a car in the garage, my son called me and said there was something moving around in the pool area, I told him it was probably nothing, they came upstairs 5 minutes later and said we're done. The second one, my son was working alone in the building at night and heard walking up the ramp, he looked and didn't see anyone, yet the walking continued and soon the door at the top opened and closed. I asked him what he did, he said I left.

My own experiences have been many. I've heard papers shuffling in my office, a door slam next to my office, bootsteps coming down the stairs, and talking.

I usually have my recorder going when I wander around the building, along with a few cameras. The experiences are almost a daily occurrence for me.

One day a customer came in to buy a bed frame and we began to talk, turns out she was part of a paranormal investigation team. She asked if they could invite some other teams to investigate, I said sure. This is my start and the start of the Haunted YMCA Rock Island.

I met some wonderful people that evening, it was very exciting for me.

It's like the spirits were happy to finally communicate with someone, they were quite active and engaging. Plenty of evidence was captured and an experiment done by Aaron G. Thompson and Madison Smith with a race with spirits resulted in a capture that has yet to be recreated.

Seeing the significance of an older well-built building I made the decision to make the building a historical landmark, and thanks to the preservation society it was made one in 2019.

The building was known in the paranormal community as The Haunted Rock Island YMCA up until the beginning of 2024 when the Y organization sent me a letter telling me I was infringing on their trademark and to stop. They also requested I cover the cornerstone and Y symbol above the door.

Thanks to my landmark status I did not have to, it is a protected building now.

Kandi Slater and I set out to figure out a new name for my beautiful building, and The Haunted Rock Island Roadhouse was what we settled on.

It has been a wonderful journey so far with many memorable experiences and hopefully many more to come.

Lisa Vinar & Kandi Slater

Chapter 1

The Mob and Rock Island, Illinois

The Mob's Shadow Over Rock Island, Illinois

Rock Island, Illinois, nestled along the Mississippi River, might appear at first glance to be a quaint Midwestern town with a rich history of industry and transportation. But beneath its serene surface lies a darker past, marked by the shadowy presence of organized crime. During the Prohibition era, Rock Island became a key player in the illegal activities that proliferated under the mob's influence, transforming the city into a hub of illicit trade and violence.

The Birth of a Criminal Haven

The story of Rock Island's entanglement with the mob begins in the 1920s, when the United States enacted Prohibition, banning the sale, production, and transportation of alcoholic beverages. This nationwide ban created a lucrative black market for alcohol, and criminal organizations across the country rushed to fill the demand. Rock Island, with its strategic location along the Mississippi River, became a prime spot for bootlegging operations.

The Rise of John Looney

One of the most notorious figures to emerge in Rock Island during this time was John Looney, a local crime boss who built an empire on bootlegging, gambling, and vice. Looney, a cunning and ruthless leader, established a network of speakeasies and illegal distilleries, ensuring a steady supply of alcohol to thirsty patrons. His control over the city's underground economy was absolute, enforced through bribery, intimidation, and violence.

Looney's influence extended beyond Rock Island, with connections to powerful mob families in Chicago and St. Louis. This alliance allowed him to operate with relative impunity, protected by corrupt officials who were more than willing to turn a blind eye in exchange for a cut in the profits.

The Looney Riots of 1912

The turning point in Rock Island's mob history came with the infamous Looney Riots of 1912. This period of intense violence was triggered by a power struggle between Looney's organization and rival gangs attempting to muscle in on his territory. The riots erupted in the streets of Rock Island, with gunfights and bombings becoming a daily occurrence.

One particularly bloody incident occurred when a rival gang attempted to assassinate Looney in broad daylight. The ensuing gunfight left several dead and many more injured, sending shockwaves through the community. Despite the chaos, Looney survived, and the failed assassination only served to cement his control over Rock Island.

The Old Rock Island Roadhouse

Central to many of the mob's activities in Rock Island was The Old Rock Island Roadhouse. This establishment, originally a legitimate business, was quickly co-opted by Looney's organization as a front for various illegal operations. The Roadhouse became a notorious gathering spot for bootleggers, gamblers, and gangsters, serving as a neutral ground where deals were made, and disputes were settled.

The Roadhouse's reputation for violence and debauchery grew, with tales of brutal fights, secret tunnels, and hidden rooms adding to its mystique. It was said that John Looney himself frequented the establishment, using its secluded location to plan his operations and conduct business away from prying eyes.

The Fall of John Looney

Despite his iron grip on Rock Island, John Looney's reign eventually came to an end. In the early 1920s, federal authorities began cracking down on organized crime, targeting bootlegging operations and corrupt officials. Looney's empire, built on a foundation of illegal activities, began to crumble under pressure.

In 1923, Looney was indicted on charges of murder, assault, and other crimes. Facing the prospect of a lengthy prison sentence, he went on the run, leaving Rock Island behind. He was eventually captured and sentenced to prison, where he spent the remaining years of his life. With Looney's downfall, the era of mob dominance in Rock Island ended, though the city's history remained forever marked by his legacy.

The Legacy of the Mob in Rock Island

Today, the story of the mob in Rock Island is a fascinating chapter in the city's history. The Old Rock Island Roadhouse, once a den of illicit activity, now stands as a testament to a bygone era. Visitors to Rock Island can still feel the echoes of the past, with many local legends and ghost stories centered around the notorious mobster and his cronies.

The mob's influence on Rock Island serves as a reminder of a time when the pursuit of profit led to widespread corruption and violence, transforming a quiet Midwestern town into a hotbed of criminal activity. The legacy of John Looney and his criminal empire continues to capture the imagination, a dark yet compelling piece of Rock Island's storied past.

Chapter 2

The History of the Old Rock Island Roadhouse

The Old Rock Island Illinois Roadhouse, a historical landmark with a storied past, was established in the mid-1800s. Initially serving as a stagecoach stop, the Roadhouse provided rest and respite for weary travelers journeying through the burgeoning town of Rock Island. Its strategic location along key trade routes made it a bustling hub of activity, attracting a diverse clientele ranging from merchants and traders to adventurers and settlers.

Early Days

Founding and Construction

The Roadhouse was constructed in 1845 by a local entrepreneur named John T. Harris. Recognizing the need for a convenient stopping point for stagecoaches, Harris built the establishment with sturdy timber and locally sourced stone. The design featured a large common area, several private rooms, and stables for horses, catering to the needs of both travelers and their steeds.

Role as a Stagecoach Stop

During its early years, the Roadhouse quickly gained a reputation as a reliable and hospitable stop. Stagecoaches would arrive regularly, bringing news, goods, and people from distant places. The common room often buzzed with conversations about current events, trade opportunities, and personal tales, creating a lively and vibrant atmosphere.

Growth and Expansion

Economic Impact

The success of the Roadhouse contributed significantly to the local economy. It became a meeting point for traders and merchants, facilitating commerce and trade in the region. As Rock Island grew, so did the Roadhouse, expanding its facilities to include additional rooms, a larger dining area, and improved stables.

Community Hub

Beyond its role as a traveler's rest stop, the Roadhouse also served as a community center. Local residents would gather for town meetings, social events, and celebrations. It became a focal point for the community, fostering a sense of camaraderie and unity among the townspeople.

Transition to a Tavern and Inn

Prohibition Era

The advent of the Prohibition era in the 1920s brought significant changes to the Roadhouse. The establishment transitioned from a simple rest stop to a tavern and inn, catering to the clandestine demand for alcohol. Secret rooms and hidden passages were constructed to evade law enforcement, and the Roadhouse became a notorious speakeasy, attracting a different kind of clientele.

Post-Prohibition

Following the repeal of Prohibition, the Roadhouse continued to operate as a popular tavern and inn. It retained its rustic charm and historical significance, drawing visitors interested in its rich past. The establishment underwent several renovations to preserve its original structure while updating its amenities to meet modern standards.

The Legend Begins

First Reports of Hauntings

As the Roadhouse aged, stories of ghostly encounters began to emerge. Visitors and staff reported strange noises, apparitions, and unexplained phenomena. These tales added an air of mystery to the establishment, attracting paranormal enthusiasts and curious tourists.

The Hat Man

Among the many ghost stories, the legend of the Hat Man stands out. Descriptions of this shadowy figure with a wide-brimmed hat became common, with numerous accounts of sightings and eerie experiences. The Hat Man's presence cemented the Roadhouse's reputation as one of Rock Island's most haunted locations. The hat man is believed to be that of mobster John Lowry.

Preservation and Tourism

Historical Landmark

Recognizing its historical and cultural significance, efforts were made to preserve the Old Rock Island Illinois Roadhouse. It was designated a historical landmark, ensuring its protection and maintenance for future generations.

Tourist Attraction

Today, the Roadhouse is a popular tourist attraction, drawing visitors from all over. Its rich history, combined with its reputation for paranormal activity, makes it a must-visit destination for history buffs and ghost hunters alike. Guided tours, historical exhibits, and themed events celebrate the legacy of this iconic establishment, keeping its stories and legends alive.

The Old Rock Island Illinois Roadhouse remains a testament to the past, a place where history and legend intertwine, inviting all who enter to step back in time and experience its unique charm and mystery.

Chapter 3

The Looney Riots of 1912

Introduction

The Old Rock Island Illinois Roadhouse, steeped in history and intrigue, witnessed numerous significant events during its existence. One of the most notable and tumultuous episodes was the Looney Riots of 1912. This violent series of clashes was a result of political corruption, labor unrest, and social tensions brewing in the early 20th century. The riots not only highlighted the deep-seated issues of the time but also left a lasting mark on the history of Rock Island and the Old Roadhouse.

Background and Causes

The early 1900s were a period of rapid industrialization and urbanization in the United States. Rock Island, with its strategic location and growing industries, was no exception. The city's workforce swelled with immigrants and rural migrants seeking better opportunities. However, this economic boom was accompanied by significant social and political challenges. Corruption was rampant, labor conditions were harsh, and the divide between the wealthy and the working class grew increasingly pronounced.

John Patrick Looney, a prominent figure in Rock Island, played a central role in the events leading up to the riots. Looney was a lawyer, politician, and gangster who wielded significant influence over the city's political and criminal landscape. He owned and operated several businesses, including the Rock Island News, a newspaper he used to further his political agenda and intimidate his rivals. Looney's operations were based out of several establishments, including the Old Rock Island Illinois Roadhouse.

Tensions escalated as Looney's grip on the city tightened. His criminal activities, including extortion, bribery, and violent enforcement, created a climate of fear and resentment. Labor unions and reformers began to push back against corruption and exploitation. The situation reached a boiling point in 1912 when Looney's actions led to a series of violent confrontations.

The Riots

The Looney Riots began as a labor dispute. Workers at a local factory, fed up with low wages and poor working conditions, went on strike. The strike quickly gained momentum, drawing support from various labor unions and reform groups. Looney, seeing the strike as a threat to his interests, decided to intervene. He hired strikebreakers and used his influence to deploy local law enforcement against the strikers.

The initial confrontations were marked by skirmishes between strikers, strikebreakers, and police. The situation rapidly deteriorated as both sides resorted to violence. The Old Rock Island Illinois Roadhouse, a known stronghold of Looney's operations, became a focal point of the conflict. Strikers and their supporters viewed the Roadhouse as a symbol of the corruption they were fighting against.

On a fateful night in August 1912, tensions exploded into full-scale riots. A large group of strikers and reformers marched towards the Roadhouse, intending to confront Looney and his associates. They were met with a fierce response from Looney's men, who were armed and prepared for a fight. The resulting clash was brutal, with gunfire, Molotov cocktails, and melee combat engulfing the area.

The riots spread quickly throughout Rock Island, with other groups seizing the opportunity to challenge Looney's dominance. Fires broke out, buildings were looted, and chaos reigned in the streets. The local police, overwhelmed and outnumbered, struggled to restore order. The National Guard was eventually called in to quell the violence.

Aftermath and Legacy

The Looney Riots of 1912 left a deep scar on Rock Island. The violence resulted in numerous deaths and injuries, as well as significant property damage. The Old Rock Island Illinois Roadhouse, once a symbol of Looney's power, was heavily damaged in the riots. Its walls, which had witnessed countless secret deals and criminal activities, now bore the marks of a violent uprising.

John Patrick Looney's influence began to wane in the aftermath of the riots. The public outcry and the increased scrutiny from state and federal authorities made it difficult for him to continue his operations with impunity. While he remained a powerful figure for several more years, his grip on Rock Island was irreparably weakened.

The riots also had a lasting impact on the labor movement and political landscape in Rock Island. The violence underscored the need for reform and greater protections for workers' rights. It led to increased efforts to curb corruption and improve labor conditions, although these changes were slow and met with resistance.

The Old Rock Island Illinois Roadhouse, despite its association with violence and corruption, became a historical landmark. It served as a reminder of a turbulent time in the city's history and the complex interplay between crime, politics, and social justice. Efforts to preserve the building and its history have ensured that the story of the Looney Riots and the Roadhouse's role in them will not be forgotten.

Conclusion

The Looney Riots of 1912 were a defining moment in the history of Rock Island and the Old Rock Island Illinois Roadhouse. They highlighted the deep-seated issues of corruption, labor exploitation, and social unrest that characterized the early 20th century. The riots, while violent and destructive, also served as a catalyst for change, prompting greater awareness and action towards addressing these problems. Today, the Roadhouse stands as a testament to this tumultuous period and the enduring struggle for justice and reform.

John Patrick Loony

Chapter 4

John Looney

John Looney and the Old Rock Island Illinois Roadhouse

Introduction

The story of John Patrick Looney and the Old Rock Island Illinois Roadhouse is a captivating tale of power, corruption, and crime in the early 20th century. Looney, a notorious mobster, lawyer, and politician, wielded significant influence over Rock Island, Illinois, and its surrounding areas. His operations were often based out of various establishments, including the infamous Roadhouse, which served as a focal point for many of his illicit activities. This account delves into the life of John Looney, his criminal empire, and the role the Old Rock Island Illinois Roadhouse played in his notorious legacy.

Early Life and Rise to Power

John Patrick Looney was born in Ottawa, Illinois, in 1865. He grew up in a modest household and pursued a career in law, graduating from the University of Michigan Law School. Looney's legal acumen and ambition quickly propelled him into the political and business circles of Rock Island. By the early 1900s, he had established himself as a prominent lawyer and influential figure in the city.

Looney's rise to power was marked by his ability to blend legitimate business practices with criminal activities. He owned and operated the Rock Island News, a newspaper that he used to further his political influence and intimidate his opponents. The paper often published sensational and scandalous stories about those who opposed Looney, effectively silencing dissent and consolidating his power.

The Old Rock Island Illinois Roadhouse

The Old Rock Island Illinois Roadhouse, located on the outskirts of Rock Island, became one of Looney's primary bases of operations. The Roadhouse was a large, imposing building that served multiple purposes: it was a speakeasy, a gambling den, and a meeting place for Looney's criminal associates. The establishment was notorious for its illicit activities and was frequented by a wide array of characters, from corrupt politicians to hardened criminals.

The Roadhouse's secluded location made it an ideal spot for conducting illegal business away from the prying eyes of law enforcement. Looney used the establishment to host lavish parties, where he entertained local officials and business leaders, further solidifying his network of influence and corruption. The Roadhouse also served as a safe haven for Looney's enforcers, who carried out his orders and protected his interests with ruthless efficiency.

Criminal Empire and Corruption

John Looney's criminal empire was built on a foundation of extortion, bribery, and violence. He controlled numerous illegal enterprises, including gambling, bootlegging, and prostitution. Looney's influence extended into the political realm, where he used his power to manipulate elections, secure lucrative contracts, and eliminate rivals. His ability to blend legitimate and illegitimate activities allowed him to maintain a veneer of respectability while engaging in widespread corruption.

One of Looney's most notorious tactics was his use of intimidation and violence to silence the opposition. His enforcers, known as "Looney's Boys," were feared throughout Rock Island. They carried out acts of arson, assault, and even murder to protect Looney's interests and maintain his grip on power. The Old Rock Island Illinois Roadhouse often served as the planning ground for these nefarious activities.

Looney's reach extended beyond Rock Island, as he forged alliances with other criminal organizations in the Midwest. He collaborated with mobsters from Chicago and St. Louis, expanding his influence and ensuring the flow of illegal goods and services. The Roadhouse was a key location for these meetings, providing a neutral ground where deals could be struck, and disputes resolved.

The Looney Riots and Decline

The Looney Riots of 1912 marked a turning point in John Looney's criminal career. The riots erupted because of labor unrest and public outrage over Looney's corrupt practices. Workers at a local factory went on strike to protest low wages and poor working conditions. Looney, viewing the strike as a threat to his interests, hired strikebreakers and used his influence to deploy local law enforcement against the strikers.

The situation quickly escalated into violent confrontations between strikers, strikebreakers, and police. The Old Rock Island Illinois Roadhouse became a focal point of the conflict, as it was seen as a symbol of Looney's power and corruption. On a fateful night in August 1912, a large group of strikers and reformers marched to the Roadhouse, intending to confront Looney and his associates. The resulting clash was brutal, with gunfire, Molotov cocktails, and melee combat engulfing the area.

The riots spread throughout Rock Island, leading to significant property damage and loss of life. The National Guard was eventually called in to restore order. The public outcry and increased scrutiny from state and federal authorities weakened Looney's grip on the city. While he remained a powerful figure for several more years, his influence was irreparably damaged.

The End of an Era

In 1922, John Looney's criminal empire began to crumble. He was indicted on multiple charges, including murder, extortion, and racketeering. The trial was a sensational affair, drawing national attention and exposing the extent of Looney's corruption. Despite his attempts to bribe jurors and intimidate witnesses, Looney was convicted and sentenced to 14 years in prison.

The Old Rock Island Illinois Roadhouse, once a bustling center of criminal activity, fell into disrepair. Its walls, which had witnessed countless secret deals and violent confrontations, stood as silent witnesses to a bygone era. The building was eventually abandoned, its legacy overshadowed by the notorious events that had unfolded within its confines.

John Looney was released from prison in 1932, but his influence had waned, and he lived out his remaining years in obscurity. He passed away in 1942, leaving behind a complex legacy of power, corruption, and violence.

Legacy and Cultural Impact

The story of John Looney and the Old Rock Island Illinois Roadhouse continues to captivate historians and enthusiasts of true crime and mob history. Looney's ability to manipulate the legal and political systems while maintaining a vast criminal empire is a testament to the complexities of early 20th-century America. His life and activities have been the subject of books, documentaries, and even folklore, highlighting the enduring fascination with his larger-than-life persona.

The Old Rock Island Illinois Roadhouse itself has become a symbol of this turbulent period. Efforts to preserve its history and architecture have ensured that the tales of corruption, violence, and intrigue associated with the building will not be forgotten. It stands as a reminder of the era when mobsters like John Looney held sway over cities, blending legitimate business practices with criminal activities in a quest for power and control.

Conclusion

John Looney's reign over Rock Island and his connection to the Old Rock Island Illinois Roadhouse illustrate a dark chapter in the city's history. His ability to navigate the worlds of law, politics, and organized crime made him a formidable figure, but also a symbol of the corruption and violence that plagued early 20th-century America. The Roadhouse, once a bustling hub of illegal activity, now stands as a historical landmark, preserving the legacy of a man whose life was marked by both ambition and infamy. The story of John Looney and the Old Rock Island Illinois Roadhouse is a testament to the enduring allure of true crime tales and the complex interplay of power, corruption, and justice.

John Looney

Wanted Poster

Chapter 5

The Spirits of the Roadhouse

Spirits of The Old Rock Island Illinois Roadhouse

The Old Rock Island Illinois Roadhouse is a storied location, steeped in both historical significance and paranormal intrigue. Over the years, it has become a hotspot for ghost hunters, historians, and those intrigued by the supernatural. The building's checkered past, involving mobsters, illicit activities, and violent confrontations, has left a lasting imprint that many believe is the source of its numerous hauntings. Here, we delve into the tales of the spirits said to haunt The Old Rock Island Illinois Roadhouse.

The Lady in White: Helen Van Dale

Perhaps the most famous spirit associated with The Old Rock Island Illinois Roadhouse is that of Helen Van Dale, often referred to as "The Lady in White." Helen's story is one of love, betrayal, and tragedy. As the legend goes, Helen was a beautiful young woman who frequented the Roadhouse during its heyday in the early 20th century. She was romantically involved with a prominent figure at the establishment, potentially John Looney or one of his close associates.

Helen met a tragic end, though the specifics vary. Some say she was caught in the crossfire during a violent confrontation; others claim she was a scorned lover who took her own life. Regardless of the details, her spirit is said to roam the halls of the Roadhouse, forever searching for peace. Visitors and staff have reported seeing a woman in a flowing white dress, her face etched with sorrow. Her apparition is often accompanied by a chilling cold and a sense of profound sadness.

The Mobster: John Looney

John Looney, a notorious mobster who used The Old Rock Island Illinois Roadhouse as a base for his operations, is another spirit said to linger within its walls. Looney was a powerful and feared figure in the early 20th century, known for his ruthless tactics and involvement in numerous criminal enterprises. His life was marked by violence, betrayal, and an unrelenting pursuit of power.

It is believed that Looney's spirit remains tied to the Roadhouse, perhaps because of his violent demise or his strong connection to the place. Witnesses have reported seeing the shadowy figure of a man dressed in early 20th-century attire, often in the basement or near areas associated with illicit activities. His presence is said to evoke feelings of dread and unease, as if his malevolent energy still permeates the building.

The Hat Man

Another chilling apparition reported at The Old Rock Island Illinois Roadhouse is that of the Hat Man. This entity is described as a tall, shadowy figure wearing a wide-brimmed hat. The Hat Man's origins and identity are unclear, but his presence is undeniably terrifying. Witnesses often report a sense of being watched, followed by a sudden, inexplicable coldness. The Hat Man is known for appearing in dark corners and then vanishing without a trace.

Some speculate that the Hat Man might be another mobster or criminal who met a violent end at the Roadhouse. Others believe he is a darker, more malevolent spirit that has been drawn to the location by its violent history. Whatever the case, the Hat Man's presence adds another layer of fear to the already haunted atmosphere of the Roadhouse. The Hat Man is believed to be the spirit of John Looney,

The Disembodied Voices

In addition to specific apparitions, The Old Rock Island Illinois Roadhouse is also known for its plethora of disembodied voices. These voices are often heard in various parts of the building, including the basement, the bar area, and the upper floors. Visitors and paranormal investigators have reported hearing conversations, whispers, and even screams, often in the dead of night when the building is otherwise silent.

One of the most common reports involves the sound of a woman's voice, believed to be that of Helen Van Dale. Her voice is often heard softly weeping or calling out a name, possibly that of her lost lover. Other voices are more indistinct, suggesting multiple spirits communicating or reliving moments from their past. These auditory phenomena contribute to the eerie and unsettling ambiance of the Roadhouse.

The Poltergeist Activity

Poltergeist activity is another commonly reported occurrence at The Old Rock Island Illinois Roadhouse. Objects are said to move on their own, doors slam shut unexpectedly, and lights flicker without explanation. Many believe this activity is the result of restless spirits attempting to communicate or express their displeasure with the living.

One particularly famous incident involved a group of paranormal investigators who visited the Roadhouse. During their investigation, a heavy table reportedly moved several inches on its own, and equipment malfunctioned repeatedly. Such incidents have been experienced by many visitors, adding to the Roadhouse's reputation as a hub of supernatural activity.

The Residual Hauntings

In addition to intelligent hauntings, where spirits interact with the living, The Old Rock Island Illinois Roadhouse is also believed to be the site of several residual hauntings. Residual hauntings are like recordings of past events that play back repeatedly, often without any interaction with the present.

One such residual haunting involves the sounds of a lively party, complete with music, laughter, and the clinking of glasses. This phenomenon is often reported late at night, long after the Roadhouse has closed. It is believed to be an echo of the many raucous gatherings that took place during the building's heyday. Another residual haunting involves the sound of gunfire and shouting, likely a replay of one of the many violent confrontations that occurred within its walls.

The Child Spirit

Adding a poignant touch to the haunted atmosphere of The Old Rock Island Illinois Roadhouse is the presence of a child spirit. Little is known about the identity or origins of this spirit, but sightings and experiences have been reported by multiple witnesses. The child is often seen playing in the corners of rooms, laughing, and sometimes crying.

Witnesses have described feeling a small hand tugging at their clothes or hearing the faint sound of a child's laughter echoing through the halls. Some believe the child may have been a victim of one of the many violent episodes that occurred at the Roadhouse, while others think the spirit might have been a resident of the building during its early years.

Conclusion

The Old Rock Island Illinois Roadhouse is a location steeped in history and haunted by numerous spirits. From the tragic figure of Helen Van Dale to the menacing presence of John Looney and the mysterious Hat Man, the Roadhouse's paranormal activity is both varied and compelling. Disembodied voices, poltergeist activity, residual hauntings, and the presence of a child spirit all contribute to the rich tapestry of ghostly lore surrounding this infamous establishment.

Whether one believes in the supernatural or not, the stories and experiences reported at The Old Rock Island Illinois Roadhouse offer a fascinating glimpse into the darker side of its history. The building stands as a testament to the lives and events that have left an indelible mark on its walls, creating a haunted legacy that continues to captivate and intrigue.

Al Capone at The Old Rock Island Illinois Roadhouse: A Tale of Intrigue and Infamy

In the annals of American history, few names evoke the same sense of intrigue and notoriety as Al Capone. The infamous gangster, who ruled Chicago's underworld during the Prohibition era, is said to have left his mark on numerous locations throughout the Midwest. Among these is The Old Rock Island Illinois Roadhouse, a storied establishment steeped in legend and lore.

The Roadhouse: A Hub of Activity

The Old Rock Island Illinois Roadhouse, situated along a key transportation route, became a popular destination during the early 20th century. Its strategic location made it an ideal spot for travelers, businessmen, and, as the stories go, bootleggers and mobsters. The Roadhouse's blend of rustic charm and discreet seclusion provided the perfect cover for illicit activities during Prohibition, when the sale and consumption of alcohol were illegal.

Al Capone's Connection

According to local legend, Al Capone frequented The Old Rock Island Illinois Roadhouse during the height of his power. It is said that Capone used the establishment as a meeting place for clandestine business dealings, leveraging its location to conduct transactions away from the prying eyes of law enforcement. The Roadhouse, with its network of hidden rooms and secret passages, offered the perfect hideaway for a man of Capone's infamy.

The Infamous Meeting

One of the most enduring tales involves a fateful meeting between Capone and a rival gang leader at the Roadhouse. The story goes that in the early 1930s, Capone arranged a secret meeting at the establishment to negotiate a truce with a competing gang. The tension was palpable as both parties arrived under the cover of night, each accompanied by heavily armed bodyguards.

Inside a private room at the Roadhouse, the two gang leaders sat across from each other, flanked by their men. The air was thick with cigarette smoke and the scent of bootleg whiskey, the very lifeblood of their criminal enterprises. Negotiations were tense, with both sides wary of a double-cross. Despite the underlying hostility, a temporary agreement was reached, allowing for a brief period of peace in the bloody gang wars that plagued the region.

The Ghostly Aftermath

The Roadhouse's association with Capone did not end with the meeting. Over the years, numerous visitors and paranormal investigators have reported strange occurrences that they attribute to the gangster's lingering presence. Witnesses have described seeing a shadowy figure dressed in 1920s attire, often spotted in the same room where the infamous meeting took place. Others have heard disembodied voices and the faint clinking of glasses, as if a spectral party were still underway.

The Legend Lives On

Today, The Old Rock Island Illinois Roadhouse stands as a monument to a bygone era, its walls steeped in history and mystery. The stories of Al Capone's visits continue to draw curious tourists and ghost hunters, each hoping to catch a glimpse of the infamous gangster's ghost. The Roadhouse remains a fascinating chapter in the larger-than-life saga of Al Capone, a place where the past seems to linger just out of reach, shrouded in shadows and whispers.

In conclusion, Al Capone's connection to The Old Rock Island Illinois Roadhouse is a tale woven from the fabric of American folklore. Whether entirely true or embellished over the years, it captures the imagination and offers a tantalizing glimpse into the secretive world of one of history's most notorious criminals. The Roadhouse, with its blend of historical significance and paranormal intrigue, continues to captivate all who walk through its doors.

Al Capone

Chapter 6

Stories from Paranormal Investigators

WINDIGO PARANORMAL

Founders: Greg & Heather Kelly

Founders notes Rock Island YMCA Illinois.

Time to hear the stories behind the investigation.

I feel like with every away investigation the task of packing the vehicle is always a task. Will it all fit? Who is going to be cramped? Lol. This one was no different. We used Lauren's vehicle this time. 5 people, one vehicle, tons of cases, coolers, and pumpkin bars.... Well of course we made it fit! I must pay homage to those dang pumpkin cream cheese bars that Kristin Koch mama made for the team. They were so good, and I believe it was our co-team we went with that said he wanted to pay respects to the baking mistress that made those. He wasn't kidding. They hit the spot more than once through the night. So huge thank you!

We always have fun and laughs on our trips, but this time was extra. We were just all so excited to get away to another cool haunted destination. This time was Rock Islands Haunted YMCA Rock Island. Built in the early 1900's. This huge block sized brick building that is ever so slightly decaying. The outside holding its own, but the inside decaying, revealing its bones and stories that lay within. 4 floors, and a basement. The inside only showing remnants of the identity it once held. A running track that appears to be falling, missing boards in its floor. A pool that is now concrete filled and just a floor. At some point this building was taken over by storage U Haul lockers. People rent lockers to store their goods. Most empty and unlocked. Currently the building is a furniture store.

To back track a little this was a collaboration ghost hunt with the Iowa Ghost Squad. Seriously a great group of people with one or two common denominators. Ghost hunting and laughs. We enjoyed our laughs with this group. They are down to earth, funny, amazing investigators. A few times we enjoyed being able to investigate with a few from their crew.

So, we arrive in Illinois and always the first order of business is finding the local crystal shop. We found it but it was NOT what we are accustomed to. So, we walked in and out. Found a cute little antique shop nearby and browsed there but bought nothing.

We asked the owners of the antique shop if there was a restaurant in the neighborhood with good food who could accommodate 15 people. So, we all met at the Mexican restaurant around the corner from the haunted location. I knew in the first few minutes we were going to love this team. They easily smiled and laughed and had such great energy. By the time dinner was over we were contemplating our next collaboration.

Then it was off to the haunted YMCA. We met the owner. She gave the newbies the fast-paced tour, only revealing the chilling stories the building was hiding. "Oh, this room is the attack room" she said, "this room is where the portal is" etc. My impression was at one point a medium had visited there and the owner trusted everything they said.

The building was huge. I must admit I wondered if my weary body would make it to all the spots in it. Lots of walking and even more stairs.

The teams went outside to grab a quick group photo. After we went out to grab our gear. We heard a gunshot that sounded like it was in front of our building, and we did see a police vehicle fly by after. The neighborhood where the building was located is in the old part of town. You could see revitalization efforts happening in the area, but it certainly had that sketchy feel to it. So right off the bat we were on edge.

We headed into the building and our first stop was the basement level. Specifically, the wrestling room. The owner would say it was "the room they hung women from the walls in".

The tails of rape, hiding bodies, a brothel, and the mafia was the undertone for most areas.

We did hear a spirit ask for "help", but anytime we tried to communicate further my impression was someone was not allowing it. We did get a male spirit to say more in the room but nothing more from the female who needed help.

I think our next stop was the workshop. At our live we asked if the spirits could say Hi to one of our viewers. We heard "Hi Carla!" So that was very cool.

We then headed to the 4th floor to the room where the teacher that liked girls, but molested boys in stayed. Next thing you know Kristin says how hot she was. It was hot up there, but I said to her it's not that bad. She looked like she had her feet to the flame's kind of hot. Then she mentions her neck is burning. Which is a telltale sign of a spirit scratch. Sure, enough she had a long thick scratch on her neck. The 4th floor was active for us. We saw shadows dart across the hallways, the doorknob rattle as if it was being turned. We had equipment go off in unoccupied rooms. We each sat alone in the "attack room", and we all had a similar experience. It was as if the room was filled up with people. It got darker. I could see black shadow people filling the room and almost enveloping me. I don't think anyone stayed in the room more than 5 min.

We headed down to the furniture show room for a snack & laugh time. We did investigate with the other team after, and again lots of equipment interaction. Near the old pool they have what some would describe as a Dexter room or an isolation room. The owner hung up black tarps and put a red bulb in the room with a mirror. Some of us tried to get lost in the mirror and do the experiment. For me it worked, but for the rest it did not.

We chose to drive home as we had hit the building hard for 6 hours of investigation. The drive home sucked. Rain and puddles made it rough. We all were happy to be in our own beds.

In Loving Memory of

Kristin Koch

Kristin Koch with Greg Kelly

Writing a paragraph for a beloved lost friend is one thing, writing it for a beloved friend and investigator is another. Paranormal teams have this unspoken bond. Like family but more. Kristin was no different. She was a hospice nurse by day, and paranormal investigator by night. Sadly, my team Windigo Paranormal lost Kristin to what we would learn was a brain aneurysm at the young age of 40. Just 18 days after our investigation at Rock Island we would suddenly lose the light of our team. Things for our team have never been the same since losing her but we do not let the memory of Kristin go by without regaling in stories about her. Her last investigation would be at Rock Island YMCA. After she passed the team wondered, and me especially, did the spirit of whatever scratched her affect her in such a way that she would pass at the young age of 40? One will never know.

Written by Heather Kelly.

Aaliyah

Organic Energy Healings in Janesville, WI.

My experience at the Haunted Rock Island Roadhouse Paracon Oct 2023, arriving at the historic building, the only inkling I had about its past was that Al Capone had frequented it and it had once served as a Y.M.C.A. Curious to explore its mysteries firsthand, I intentionally avoided any historical research, hoping to allow my intuition to paint the picture. A group of us went to the basement, guided by Kandi Slater and accompanied by a small group of fellow psychics, our mission was to tap into our intuitive senses and discover the unseen. The basement was dimly lit, and the past wanted to share its story with us. Standing in the room, an unsettling yet intriguing sensation washed over me. In the corner of the room, I felt a distinct presence. My right hip began to throb with an ache that wasn't my own, and a vision formed in my mind's eye: a man with a cane, moving with a deliberate, albeit labored, pace. I realized this pain belonged to a janitor who had once walked these very floors. Simultaneously, another member of our group picked up on a female presence. As I tuned in, a vivid image emerged—a woman who wore beautiful brooch that seemed to glimmer with its own light. The brooch appeared to be an important detail, and we began piecing together that the janitor and the woman were likely connected in some significant way. The atmosphere grew more charged with our collective impressions, and we soon sensed the presence of a young boy, whose spirit seemed to linger somewhere behind a nearby wall it felt like he couldn't breathe. Kandi confirmed our findings, the historical revelations sent a chill down my spine. The janitor with the limp and cane who was romantically involved with the woman wearing the brooch and she managed the brothel that was there at that time. The brooch was an artifact of hers, and the tragic story of the young boy who had drowned in the pool when it was the Y.M.C.A.

As we left the basement and stepped into the hallway, a curious sight caught my eye: a punching bag was swaying gently in a small, deliberate circle. It seemed almost hypnotic, like a pendulum measuring out time and space in its slow, rhythmic motion. The movement was so serene and yet so out of place that it added a surreal final touch to our exploration. After investigating the basement, I decided to explore further and made my way upstairs to a room known as "the trunk room." When I entered, I found four people already settled in, their array of equipment glowing softly in the dim light. I asked if I could join them, and they happily allowed me to join their session. I took a seat and closed my eyes, attempting to open my senses to the room's energy. Almost immediately, I was struck by an overwhelming sense of malevolence. The atmosphere was thick with a dark, chaotic energy, as if the room itself was recoiling from past violence. My intuition led me to a disturbing vision: a violent confrontation had unfolded here. I saw in my mind's eye two men and a woman who seemed terrified. One man's intent was clearly sinister—he wanted to harm her, to violate her in a way that went beyond simple cruelty. The other man, however, seemed to have feelings for her and couldn't take any more of the violence that he had witnessed, there was a lot of evil that he had witnessed. The vision became more vivid as I saw the confrontation, the struggle was brutal, and the violence was palpable. It ended with the death of the man who could no longer stand by and watch the evil down to so many women. In the hallway outside the room, I sensed that the man met his death, it felt like he was thrown down the elevator shaft. I later learned that the room indeed was used for sinister purposes and more than one life was taken in that very room, the trunks were used to carry out the dead bodies and tossed in the river, and a man who was overwhelmed and fearful of all the violence was brutally beaten and murdered. The building had so many other secrets to share. My Name is Aaliyah, I am with Organic Energy Healings in Janesville, WI.

We Are Paranormal

Co-Founder Nathan Hopwood

Stories of Rock Island Roadhouse.

We have filmed here a few times, and this place holds a special place in my heart. Lisa has always treated me well and like I am a part of the family So, some stories I remember, one of them was in the trunk room. A member of the team was inappropriately touched, and it sent our Bugsy box into a frenzy. I got mad and yelled at the spirits and let them know how unhappy I was. The Bugsy box was going crazy. Making noises I had never heard come out of the back box. When I got close to the end of yelling at the spirits. I said so knock off your bullshit, the Bugsy Box went back to normal. Another time when

    We were filming. We had two people have a conversation. A man and a woman had an argument. We asked if anyone needed any help. A woman said "yes" then a man said sternly "No"! The woman then responded with a very loud "Fuck Yourself" then another man's voice comes through and says, "Uh Oh"! The room with all the mirrors by the pool area is an active portal.

I got proof of that when a spirit from another location came through and communicated with us. She made it known where she was from and her name. Every level has different energy on it. It is truly on another level as far as paranormal activity.

We were filming with Nick Simons and Aaron G Thompson, and we were doing a spirit box session. We asked about the owner and the response came through "John Looney is a Bitch!" They also said "hey there beautiful" to a woman as she removed her sweatshirt while we were filming as well. This was all on the 4th floor.

Every time I go there it is another experience in a different area. Great location a must see for any paranormal investigator.

Nathan Hopwood: Co-Founder We Are Paranormal.

Rob Walczak

Owner of Ghost Gear

The Bed

I assisted Allen Cornelison with a live stream from our on-site location. We set up base camp in
the room between the stairwells, where the office furniture is located—it seemed fitting. While
Allen conducted a solo investigation, I remained at base camp. Allen reported hearing voices
from the basement, and they were clearly audible on the video—quite loud, in fact. As Allen
pursued these voices, I began to hear voices in the stairwell behind me. It felt as if someone
had broken in, and I realized we might not be alone. When I opened the stairwell door, I
distinctly heard someone say, "You should be outside, it's nice outside. " At that moment, I was
convinced someone else was in the building. When Allen returned from his solo investigation,
We thoroughly searched the building from top to bottom but found no one. The only way in was

through the front door, which was locked and had an open-door chime. The rear door was
barricaded.

Voices

After a night of investigation, we decided to take a nap on one of the beds. Above us, we heard
the clattering and dragging of heavy objects, as if someone were moving an old school lunch
table across the floor. As the noise subsided, I began to doze off. Suddenly and forcefully, my
bed moved and shook, startling me awake. I called out to Allen, who was with me. When he
came over, he noticed the bed was crooked and had moved away from the wall in the direction I
felt the impact. While I can't say for certain if the bed was already like that, given how far it was
from the wall, my OCD would have likely noticed and corrected it earlier.

From The Ashes Paranormal

Co-founder Kandi Slater

Uncovering the Secrets of Rose

I am the co-founder of From the Ashes Paranormal with my husband, Derek. We have frequently investigated the Rock Island Roadhouse since 2018. To this day, this remains one of the most active locations we have been to. I can honestly say we have never been there and not had an experience. Derek and I have had many memorable moments here. On our first visit, I and two friends were chased up the stairs to the 4th floor by an entity. We could literally hear the footsteps running after us. That was all it took, and I was in love with this location!

We have had many memorable moments here. Some that made us laugh, like the time we asked mobster John Looney, what he thought of Al Capone, and very clearly over Necrophonics he replied, "He's a pussy." Or the time Lisa, Wendy, Josey, Derek and I were setting up for our first paracon and the balloons that were on the balloon arch and on the floor would mysteriously pop, making us jump. We could not figure out why the balloons were randomly just popping, that was until Derek and another medium present were laughing and explained to us what they were seeing. They were seeing Paul Lowman, the kid who drowned in the pool. Paul was

putting his finger up to his mouth, saying "shhhhhhh." He would then pop a balloon, watch us jump, and run off laughing.

Some have made us jump. I'll always remember being up on the fourth floor with a first-time investigator, closing a door, only to have it open itself, creaking loudly as it opened.

Some have made us want to cry. There was a visit by a woman who died at home on the property by drinking poison before the YMCA purchased the property. Then of course there is the story of Rose.

One of my most memorable experiences at the Roadhouse was in the old wrestling room in the basement. On a cool fall October evening, Derek and I were investigating the building for the sole purpose of trying to communicate with the spirit of a woman who had taken a liking to me since the first time I communicated with her.

Backstory: One evening a woman, we would later learn to be named Rose, appeared to a medium, indicating that she wanted to be followed. The medium followed her to the wrestling room where she showed him how she was chained to a wall in the back of the room. Upon turning on the lights, the metal rods that held the chains were still in fact in the wall. Between that night and this evening Derek and I had visited with the woman. Derek, being a medium, was able to see that she wanted to communicate. She showed herself chained to the wall and being forced to be one of the notorious Helen Van Dales ladies of the night. He saw her repeatedly being beaten and sexually abused. I would try to communicate with her in a soft gentle tone. Derek and the World Renowned medium, Kathrine Sorilos who was joining us remotely from Greece indicated she was very taken with me.

Fast forward to this evening Our mission was to make contact with the woman and find out who she was and her story. To set up for the investigation we set up not only an audio and video recorder. I was tied to the wall like the way this woman had shown Derek. I was also blind folded and had headphones with Necrophonics on it with the volume turned all the way up. Cat balls were placed on each side of my feet and in front of me about a foot away. A periscope was set between me and the doorway. Derek also had a phone with Necrophonics playing.

Once we were set up, Derek turned out the lights, and stood in the back of the room as not

To set of any equipment. A few minutes into the session Derek whispered, "she's here." Keep in mind I could not hear anything Derek was saying as he was whispering. I would later hear these comments on the recordings. He then said, "she's heading towards Kandi." Seconds later, the lights on the periscope lit up, heading in my direction. Moments later I said, "it's getting cold on my right side." At the same time, unbeknownst to me the cat ball on my right went off.

Just as Derek began to say that the woman was touching my hair I said, "It feels like someone, or something is petting my hair."

Derek whispered, "I'm Derek and this is my wife, Kandi. If you remember us, can you let us know." The word yes came over Derek's Necrophonics, just as the cat ball in front of me went off.

Derek whispered, "Can you tell us your name?"

"Rose" was heard over Necrophonics, and seconds later I said, "Rose."

My hands began hurting so I said, "My hands hurt." Over Dereks the words "help her" came

out loud and clear. Derek whispered "She's moving to the other side and trying to get her hands

out of the rope. The cat ball to my front, then left began going off. I then said, "My left side is getting very cold, especially my hand."

The words "Help her." Come over Necrophonics again. At this point Derek turns on the light, takes off my blindfold and unties me. He told me that Rose was getting very upset and worried about me.

We continued the investigation with the lights on, cat balls and Necrophonics. Unfortunately, we could not get Rose's last name, however, we confirmed her name was Rose and determined she was most likely there in the 1920's. She communicated that she was afraid of the men who would come in the room and "violate" her and "take it." If she failed to perform, we were beaten.

We were told he was led there by Helen with the promise she would have a better life but was locked in this room. Throughout the whole session it felt as though Rose was playing with my hair, and trying to comfort me, which Derek was able to confirm. We concluded the session by thanking her for spending time with us and letting her know we would not forget her.

Recently we added a mirrors room in the area that was the pool when the building was a YMCA. This room is quickly becoming a favorite of many investigators. Lisa and I experienced how active this room is. Before the rooms were added, Lisa and I went down to the room to have a quick session. It was a hot spring evening and the temperature in this room was perfect.

As we sat on the floor with our GS2 laser grid, Epoch Box and recorder we immediately knew we were not alone. We could hear voices having conversations on the other side of the wall, when the only other person in the building was Derek, who was asleep upstairs.

The entities in the room were answering questions on one of my personal all-time favorite pieces of equipment, the Epoch Box. It started getting cold in the room and Lisa and I began feeling nauseous. On the display of the laser grid, the cold spots were showing on the ceiling.

We sat back and watched for a while, listening to the voices. Slowly it looked as though something snake like was moving across the ceiling, matching movements and cold spots that were showing on the laser grid.

As we watched the snake-like formation on the ceiling move and occasionally come down, we grew increasingly nauseous and got terrible headaches.

We decided that it was best to call it a night. I could go on and on with stories of incredible experiences from this amazing building, but I think you should experience it yourself!

Kandi Slater

Shadow Hunters Paranormal Investigators & Events

Founder: Deidre Sanford

Psychic Medium, Holistic Therapy Provider

Rock Island Roadhouse October 2024 During my initial visit to the Rock Island Roadhouse in October 2024 I had no idea what to expect. I had heard from others in the paranormal community that the building was haunted and the information I had ended there. I was quite comfortable having less knowledge than others; I prefer to build my own stories based on personal experience. Was I aware it was previously a brothel, hotel and originally a YMCA? Did I know this paranormal convention was taking place in a present-day furniture store? I absolutely know all those things and had accepted them as fact. What I didn't know it how I would feel during my first tour of the building. So, I loaded up my car and headed for Rock Island, IL to learn firsthand what this building, and its ghostly inhabitants, would choose to reveal.

As my GPS guided me through the town of Rock Island, I remember feeling my way past many houses which gave off the haunted vibe and the old YMCA did not feel much different. Did it make the hair on the back of my neck? No, but that rarely happens to me; I typically more of a knowing something here is different. This feeling certainly applied to this building as I deliberately unfolded myself from my vehicle, yanked tubs from my trunk, hand headed up to the back loading door.

As I navigated the ramps peering around corners, I couldn't help but feel others peering back curious to meet yet another new arrival. And boy did they have me pegged! I was feeling more than a little apprehensive and vulnerable as I walked deeper into the area not really knowing which way to go or how to find my way. I quite suddenly realized truly had no idea what to expect once spent more time getting settled and wandering the main floor, stairwells, and the basement. There was an unmistakable

air of excitement, anticipation, and a dash of stress as everyone zipped about preparing for the first convention to be held within these walls and the spirits were anxious to get acquainted with the arrivals.

I had been walking around knowing, sensing and seeing things others couldn't for most of my life. I would follow my intuition as I was beckoned up the stairs at The Crescent Hotel only to run back downstairs in a hurry. I had heard the tittering of young women in the dining room and been walking around all manner of places inadvertently coming upon those who were just as startled as I to be seen, but this weekend would be different. I had spent dedicated time learning to sharpen and get comfortable with my inherent abilities over the past year and was now choosing to consciously enter a building that others, with more focused experience than I, had deemed to be haunted. Eventually it came time for the building tour. I'm not sure what I believed would happen, but I wanted to see the rest of this huge building yet remained a bit timid to find out what, or who, was contained within these walls.

Kandi, our tour guide, cheerily pointed out the different areas of the main floor, pointed up stairway explaining where they would lead should we venture that way, and we finally got to the basement stairs where the workshops and a few vendors would be located. As we walked through the main areas, we approached a smaller, darker room which clearly had not been set up for the event. Kandi stood in the doorway as the 5 of us entered the space, the energy shifted, the air became somewhat still, and we stood looking at each other awkwardly as we each began to have and then share our own experiences. Someone else began to speak about what they sensed and to describe those whom we believed to be from another time they believed to be in space with us.

Rock Island Roadhouse October 2024

I don't believe any of us had prior knowledge of those we shared space with, but the descriptions began to pour forth as we compared our impressions. I had no idea the tour would include sharing these mediumship impressions and eventually became comfortable enough to share what I heard, saw and knew while in the space adding that the word I heard for a male who was with us was "caretaker" confirming Karly's impression of this man's role. He seemed to be enjoying the recognition he was receiving because in life he was not always accepted by others; he seemed to have a bit of a limp and to

be good at his work yet was consistently awkward by the social standards of the time He seemed to be a perfect fit for his role here and would likely have been considered "a bit challenged" today yet was simply different from others yet was valued for his tinkering and repair skills in his time.

The energy shifted yet again, and a female presence made herself known in the space. I could see a woman with her hair gathered behind and atop her head. The others began to share their impressions of this woman first then I, still not used to discussing such things with others, gathered my words and began to join the chat adding that I could sense the woman she was describing wearing a high collared blouse and jacket adding she had a sneaky sense of humor stating she could seem almost demure when she chose to be. She invited me to sit and continued to be quite curious about me! I was shocked as no one else I had encountered in similar circumstances had seemed to consider me the way she had. I was aware I was being assessed! She could appear rather demure and not stating there was a more raucous personality behind that exterior which was reserved for those she knew more personally. Here general energy was warm and inviting, calming too in a way yet there was more that would flash in those eyes as though we dare not anger her because she could get her dander up if needed. There were two sides to this woman, yet provocation was needed; she was a protector of others, and you best not step out of line. She was kind in her approach as I felt her draw nearer and invited me to take a seat; I sat but wasn't sure why I had been invited. She seemed to be accustomed to those who felt awkward, vulnerable and felt just a tad out of place and kept her distance fading off into the background quickly.

Deidre Sanford

All Out Paranormal

Fonder: Rex Nielson

Over the past few years of incredible investigations at the Rock Island Roadhouse I have had many personal experiences. One of my most memorable experiences was an event that on each floor we had a specialist that would take a group of 5 to 6 people at a time and share their knowledge over the years of paranormal investigating.

I was on the 2nd floor of the Roadhouse sharing my knowledge of taking pictures or Spirit Photography. I had just received a camera from Sony who had been so awesome to make my camera into a full spectrum camera with a tilting screen on it. This was my first time using the camera and was very excited to use it and share it with the groups on how it worked.

Over the course of the day, I would explain how I personally went about taking pictures in my investigations. Which was taking at least 5 pictures in a row of the same spot. Not just random pictures here and there. You will get better results when focusing on one area at a time. I also would be explaining to them how a full spectrum camera works. A full spectrum camera can take a picture in any kind of light. So, this made it a very nice piece of equipment to use when doing a paranormal investigation.

I spent that day explaining my knowledge of Spirit Photography. I took 109 pictures down the hallway over the day.

The next day when I was home and reviewing evidence. I was shocked and so excited at what I had captured with the camera. Picture 106 had a full body apparition. It looks like a clown which was significant because the Roadhouse was connected to the circus in its long history. This is the picture I captured that day. I am looking forward to many more investigations in the future. The Haunted Rock Island Roadhouse never disappoints. She has a story to share with everyone.

Rex Nielson

Karlie Bird

Psychic Medium

I was with a group of people investigating 4th floor of the building when someone else was up there provoking this spirit called Dean, it seemed like the provoker had some personal issue with Dean, the provoker was feeling sick, I touched him on his shoulder to get his attention, when he turned around i saw Dean's face on top of the provokers face. I backed away quickly from the man, he yelled at Dean asking him "is that all you got?" the spirit retaliated by "caining" us all who were in the area. It started as a slight burning sensation in the middle of my back and started to not only travel down my back but also all the way down my legs. As soon as I heard the provoker say, "fuck you Dean", I knew it was best to leave this person alone and leave the floor we were on.

As I was being walked around the building, I could feel women being assaulted in many ways and thrown down a well or a shaft of some kind, I could feel how they just felt like trash, like nothing. In life Dean was a hard man, I felt though when he was alone, he was very lonely and to fill

the void, he would with women. I feel even in death he is still a hard man and doesn't see what he did in life as "bad".
Karlie Bird Psychic Medium.

Rick Hayes

The Strap and The Blood
By
Rick Hayes
Psychic Medium/Life Coach

Not every old building, historic residence, or location a Psychic Medium enters will create a feeling of a spirit or what is defined as ghosts. Upon entering the Rock Island Roadhouse in Rock Island, Illinois, I immediately knew that this was one place spirit connections were going to happen. What I was not anticipating were the type of messages that I was going to receive.

My assistant and I traveled approximately six hours as I was invited to be the keynote speaker at an event held in the memorable multi-story building. Road weary but excited, we arrived a day early to
prepare for the weekend conference. As we pulled into the parking lot I expressed to my assistant,

"Wow, I am already liking this place." Still setting in our vehicle and admiring the brick-and-mortar structure in front of us, she replied "Are you already getting something?" My assistant knew my life given abilities not just as a Psychic Medium but also as a brother. For the past twenty plus years she has been my assistant but most of all, a loving sister. We had traveled the country and experienced many locations defined as 'haunted or active in spirit.' She knew when I had that look, those in spirit were near and the Rock Island Roadhouse was no exception.

This was our first site of the Roadhouse. Let me take a minute to clarify one of my requests when a request is asked for me to visit a location. I asked not to be told of any background history regarding the location, nor of any paranormal experiences. While visiting a location, I will be guided and communicate with those in spirit about the place. As I often share, who better to tell me the history and memories of a location than those who lived, worked, or experienced the location. Those in the body of spirit are your 'tour guides'.

We closed our vehicle doors and proceeded up the outdoor metal stairway to the steel entry door. We walked into the Roadhouse; I could smell the years of a musty aroma. The large room we were standing in appeared weathered yet solid in construction, The evidence of an exciting weekend was prominent, as several vendors had already arrived with their products proudly being displayed.

A few seconds later a greeting smile approached us and introduced herself. "Hi Rick, I'm Kandi, it is so great to finally get to meet you!" My sister and I had been corresponding with Kandi for several months finalizing agreements and presented opportunities, but this was the first time we had met in person, after a few minutes of enjoyable conversation Kandi stated "I want you to meet Lisa, She is the owner and this building actually occupies her family furniture store here."

We proceeded around a corner and entered yet another large room and approached a petite lady who were busy moving chairs. Now one thing I would like to let you know is that during this whole time I was feeling and hearing those in spirit. I have been often asked "Rick, what is your day like seeing and hearing those in spirit? Is it going on all the time?" Actually, it is. I know I was born with these spiritual abilities and for me it is a normal part of life. Those in spirit respect and understand for me to learn life, I too must experience life. Although they are always around us, they also respect to not be constant in
presence,

With that being said, the presence of those in spirit was being acknowledged, and I was receiving tremendous pulls to visit an upper floor as I passed a door. After an exchange of hugs and welcome from the Roadhouse owner Lisa, I made a request, "Would it be possible for us to go to a certain upper floor? I am being told to go there and 'learn some things". Lisa and Kandi looked at one another with a slight expression of excitement and almost replied in unison, "Yes you can!" Kandi directed us to the very same door that I felt pulled to as my sister and I followed her up another flight of metal stairs to another floor of the building. The communication was about to begin.

We were standing in a small foyer on either the third or fourth floor. I am not completely positive on which floor I was on simply because when connecting with spirit minute details are overshadowed by the words of direction being spoken by those in spirit. As the daylight cascaded through a window, I noticed in front of where we were standing was a wooden rail about waist high and what appeared to be caged wiring for protection from falling into the obvious deep shaft.

"I am being told to be careful. Life was taken here from a fall to the bottom. He (the one in spirit) was abruptly pushed and life here in physical body ended." I stated to the group. There was a silence in the air for a few minutes, then Kandi shared "You are right, Rick". I smiled and responded, "No he is right". We stood in the small entryway for several more minutes, but I did not receive any additional connection. I was beginning to think that my pull to visit this floor was for this purpose. Boy was I wrong on that assumption, for yet another person in spirit wanted to tell me about a completely different life experience.

As we stood in the foyer, I immediately heard "Come into this room, I have something to show you." I looked over to my right and noticed a small opening without a door, or with a door that was completely opened. I did not pay attention to this detail as I was focused on what I was told in spirit. I walked into the dimly lit and musty room and noticed a few boxes that were being stored and several folding chairs placed in a semi-circle position. My thoughts were "Oh, they must have had a paranormal group
investigating with equipment in this room for a reason." This was not the first time that I have visited an

'active' location with evidence of previous 'ghost hunters' who had checked out the place for possible connections.

I stood in the doorway of this room in an immobile state as Rhonda broke the silence with "Are you getting something?" My reply was what she had seen many times for many years. I heard her question yet did not hear her question, for I was focused on what I was being shown (I define it as a spirit visual) and what was being stated to me by those in spirit. I simply responded with "Yes".

Now understand that I personally do not go into a trance or start speaking in a different tone as what I define as 'Hollywood to get attention' mannerisms. I leave that up to those who ham for the media. I simply just listen.

I proceeded into the room slowly, again with a pull being guided to the back of the room. The concrete walls were cold and drab, giving the feeling of uneasiness. As I stood along the back wall, a female voice in spirit said, "look down". As my 'spiritual eyes' gazed down to the cold concrete floor, I could see the droplets of dark red blood. I was not afraid as the lady in spirit had a voice almost peaceful and must admit with a bit of a sexy tone. "If we angered her, we would be beaten here" the voice shared. I was confused yet even more curious.

I listened quietly for a few more minutes then asked, "What more do you wish for me to know?" Patiently waiting for a few more seconds she replied "look at the wall" whereupon I was pulled to look at one wall of the room to my left. What I saw once again confused me, for there were what appeared to be leather strap marks crusted in blood on the wall. "What is this?" I silently asked. The lady replied "It is what happened here. I am ok now". I felt a sensation of peaceful release and the next thing I knew she said, "thank you" in which I responded with "Thank you for sharing this with me".

I began sharing with Kandi and Rhonda the messages and visuals I had been given in as much detail as I had retained. I will always remember the look on Kandi's face when sharing the conversation. With a look of fascinating awe, she began telling Rhonda and I about the room and what history had supposedly dictated. Apparently at one time a 'Madame' ran a type of business described back many years ago as a brothel. Her reputation was said to be cold and sinister. Her 'ladies of the evening' feared her and it is said even the men were afraid of her. It was said that if one of her girls went against her demands or even became pregnant with child, that lady was beaten or may even 'disappear 'for good. The room we were standing in was supposedly where ladies were severely tortured for punishment, I listened to the background story being told to me and felt a plethora of emotions. I felt sadness for those who experienced these extremely harsh life experiences and choices. I felt a bit of anger for what had been done to one human being by another. Yet the emotion of care, love, and peace as felt from the lady in spirit who had guided me into this room. She was in her next life now and had found that peaceful love filled life not experienced in this life. All was good. As Rhonda and I enjoyed the event weekend with friends, every so often throughout the weekend I saw or felt those in spirit manifesting a glimpse of us spending time in a building filled with history and memories. Once or twice during that weekend I could also feel the energy of that spirit with the peaceful and slightly sexy voice…

A new friend.

Rick Hayes - *Psychic Medium/Life Coach*
www.lifesgift.com
Facebook: www.facebook.com/RickHayesLifesGift
Amazon Author Page: amazon.com/author/rickhayes
Podcast: **BElieve with Rick Hayes**
BElieve

From The Ashes Paranormal

Denise Brubaker

It was New Years Eve 2023 as I and a group of people were investigating the boiler room at the time. We were using the flashlight method to communicate with who we think was Helen VanDale. We asked if she was there, and the flashlight lit up. I also asked if she would like to hire me as one of her workers, she lit it up! So, I guess I'm suited for the job because she liked our interview.

Haunted Happy Hour

President & CEO: Lili Santillan

Echoes of the Rock Island Roadhouse: Haunting Encounters

By Lili Santillan | President & CEO
Haunted Happy Hour, Inc.

While the outside of the building now proudly displays the name "Dan Vinar Furniture Co.," the Haunted Rock Island Roadhouse, built in 1912, is renowned for its inexplicable tales and strange happenings.

The building's storied history includes a range of paranormal occurrences—from chilling apparitions to unexplained noises—that have left many questioning the boundary between the living and the supernatural. These fascinating rumors and spine-tingling legends were what initially drew my team and I to this mysterious location. We were eager to delve into the stories that had become local lore and uncover some of the truths behind the building's haunted reputation for ourselves.

True to its legendary notoriety, the Rock Island Roadhouse didn't hold back. From the very first moment we stepped inside, it was clear that the building was eager to demonstrate its unexplained phenomena.

Over the course of three separate investigations, we had the opportunity to witness and document some of our most memorable and chilling moments. Each visit to the Rock Island Roadhouse brought with it a fresh wave of eerie encounters. And each investigation added layers to the narrative, providing new insights and deeper understanding of the building's mystery-filled past. The building seemed to reveal its secrets gradually, as if inviting us to uncover its hidden stories.

During our first investigation, we explored the building carefully, taking our time to familiarize ourselves with each different space – learning every step and every corridor. That initial walk-through admittedly started out pretty slow; we can't say that we encountered anything that we could definitively label as paranormal.

However, when we reached the third floor, we began to wander through what seemed like a series of long hallways, stretching almost endlessly in both directions. It was here, at the beginning of what we would later discover to be a particularly active corridor, that we set up our equipment and began an EVP (Electronic Voice Phenomena) session.

With our recorders rolling and our anticipation growing, we focused our attention straight down the hallway. Suddenly, and almost gradually, a shadowy silhouette of what appeared to be a man walked across a window bathed in moonlight at the end of the hallway. The sight was brief but unmistakable, and the figure seemed to glide with an eerie grace.

We were all transfixed, unable to tear our eyes away as the silhouette moved silently, but quickly past the window. The sight of a moving apparition was a first for us, and the realization that we had just witnessed something so extraordinary left us pretty stunned. This encounter marked the beginning of our deepening fascination with the Rock Island Roadhouse.

During our second visit to the building, we captured our most unexplainable evidence to date. This time, my investigation partner was solely my teammate Vanessa. Having already explored the building once before and having researched some of the history of the building, we knew we wanted to focus some of our time in the basement, specifically in the area where the old swimming pool once was.

While in the old pool room, we encountered the usual cold spots and saw the trip wire lit up in response to our questions. However, it wasn't until two days later that we fully grasped the extent of what we had captured.

As we conducted our evidence review, we worked our way through reviewing the three recorders we had rolling for the EVP sessions. It soon became clear that one recorder had picked up something that the other two had not.

Upon reviewing the recordings, we found that for 1 minute and 47 seconds, one recorder captured the usual ambient room noise and our questions, just like the other two. However, suddenly, the recorder fell completely silent. Although it was still being recorded, the familiar background noise disappeared. Instead, we were left with an eerie, pitch-black quiet, followed by a metallic rumble and the sound of water dripping in a strangely muffled environment—almost like the underwater sensation one gets when your hearing becomes subdued. Then, almost as quickly as that shift into this oddly otherworldly environment happened, the recorder seemingly snapped back out, bringing us back into that ambient room with the familiar noise and we heard the completion of an EVP session question.

This capture gave us chills. I always say, I don't know what it sounds like to step through a portal, but I do think this recording gave us a glimpse. The abrupt shifts and cuts at the beginning and end of the recording are truly puzzling. We've since shared the recording to get others' opinions, and the consensus is that it's unexplainable.

Since that investigation, I've just been drawn back time and time again. During one of my more recent times in the building, I was with my team, Haunted Happy Hour—consisting of myself, Vanessa Iles, and Sara King. We decided to take a break from working and take a breather by just walking throughout the building. We ended up on the second floor in what used to be one of the classrooms. We sat down in the darkness, casually talking about our day and the plans we

had coming up. Suddenly, we heard the distinct creak of one of the doors out in the hallway opening and then the shuffling of footsteps walking down towards us. We were the only ones on that floor.

Since those investigations, we've been lucky to spend a lot of time in the building. We've encountered many unusual knocks, strange photo captures – like one that looks like my teammate Vanessa's face is morphing into someone else, and just simply other odd occurrences.

One of my favorite experiences with the Roadhouse was the surprising involvement of its spirit in crafting our specialty coffee blend for the Haunted Rock Island Roadhouse. Remarkably, the resident spirits, John Looney and Helen Van Dale, played a crucial role in the blend's creation. Working alongside Lisa Vinar, we explored various flavors, and both spirits made their presence known. Helen, in particular, had a distinct influence in shaping the final selection, making the process truly unforgettable.

Our experiences here in the building have been both thrilling and at times unnerving, reinforcing the building's reputation as a hotspot for paranormal activity. It's clear that the Rock Island Roadhouse is more than just a backdrop for investigations—it's an active participant in the haunting narrative we're all eager to uncover.

Lili Santillan

Eternal Paranormal

Members: Alisha, Derek, Tiffany and Charles

Eternal paranormal, established in 2022 is a local quad cities team that includes team leader Alisha McFadden, followed by Derek, Tiffany and Charles, investigating highly active paranormal buildings and homes all across the Mid-West.

On July 27th, 2024, Eternal Paranormal visited the Rock Island Roadhouse with Shawn Ellis from Eternal ex wolf pack paranormal and Tom Sappington.

We all started off the night by grouping together and talking and getting all of our equipment set up as Shawn pulls Derek aside to go downstairs in what Derek calls the "Vortex room." They get down to the room and just sit in complete darkness using no equipment, just their bodies and senses and suddenly Shawn hears a little girl's voice, followed by footsteps coming towards them down the long hallway the footsteps stop. They rushed out of the room to find out what was down there with them, and they found nobody. They both rush back upstairs to find the rest of the group in the same spot they were in when Shawn and Derek let this all happen just in the matter of 10 minutes.

Tom was telling Tiffany and Alisha about a little girl spirit that roams the building prior to the events that took place in the basement. Later on that night the group was in the back room on the main floor when suddenly Alisha saw what looked to her like feet running around the beds. She asked if a spirit wanted to play hide-n-seek and the epoch box responded "yes" so she picks the epoch box and plays the hot and cold game she tells the spirit to respond with Green for "hot" red for "cold" as she got closer to the spirit it would hit yes on the epoch box and when the activity started to dissipate the epoch box would stop like it ran off.

The same night Tiffany, Shawn and Alisha went to the second floor when the flashlight started to dim out during an evp burst session, so she asked if it was the spirit that was playing hide-n-seek earlier and if so to use the flashlight to respond and it went dim again. Then suddenly they heard a loud metal noise down the hall, so Alisha goes to check it out she yells for Derek and Tom but no response.

As they were up on the 3rd floor communicating with intelligent spirits that had quite a story to tell. Tom and Derek were very surprised with what they were getting on the Eternal box 2.0 they were both getting direct communication with what they believe to be a male spirit possible wrestler and a female spirit that could have been a working girl from the early 1900s. In conclusion each one of them has had a personal experience that leads them to wanting to come back to the Haunted Rock Island Roadhouse.

Eternal Paranormal

Haunted Explorations and Research Team

(H.E.A.R.T)

Co-Founder: Jessica Marie Proctor

Abyssal Lurker

I would like to begin with this fact in mind. None of us are Experts. So, allow me to introduce myself. My name is Jessica Marie Proctor. Those who know me, call me Jess...The pleasure is all mine. I have been a firm believer in the paranormal since I was 7 years old. For most of my life, I have always endured one type of haunting or another. Nightmares have consumed my sleep since the first night I encountered a Shadow man that I came face to face with, at such a young age. I am 32 now, and facing my fears of such entities with my team alongside me. H.E.A.R.T. Stands for Haunted Explorations and Research Team. A team I Co-Founded in the year of 2018. Along my ventures, I have encountered very fascinating individuals. Such as the ones who invited me, and my Husband Garth Proctor to The Rock Island Roadhouse in Rock Island, Illinois. I met them at an event in Vinton Iowa, during an investigation that helped validate my belief in not only the Paranormal, but what I consider Spiritual Psychology. To be Psychic.

They took a liking to my Husband and I, which brings us to this story that I share with you. Kandi and her Husband Derek Slater invited us to her Birthday Party, which just so happened to take place at Rock Island Roadhouse. My Husband and I was pretty excited, so of course we couldn't refuse. We prepped and packed our stuff, then set out for Illinois.

Upon arrival, my impressions were distasteful to say the least. Not because of the building itself, but the ones around it boxing such a place's history within. It felt congested on the outside. Inside? Took on a similar feeling, and more. Despite the place being spacious. It still felt very congested, as if the walls were hiding many secrets.

Possibly dark ones... It certainly piqued my curiosity to explore. We met with the owner of the building, Lisa. A very kind woman I might add. We set our stuff down and began to venture with our lovely guide Kandi Slater. She wanted insight on what I could feel. Did I mention I'm Psychic as well? It's not as magical as it sounds, I assure you. It's merely energy with information waiting to be felt, and to be heard.

I recall three places within that building that spoke to me. The walls echo with malicious information. Why did I feel like someone had been hurt in the basement? Specifically, a woman? Or why did I sense there had been falling near the elevator shaft? Are these remnants of my subconscious warning me this could happen to anyone in locations like this? Or is it something else, entirely?

After she gave us a short tour and I gave her my impressions, my Husband and I set out to do a little private investigation of our own. Our first stop was on the fourth floor. It felt like prison cells down each hall. The heavy doors concluded that feeling. One room with a red door, at the back end near the elevator shaft. That was the room of our choosing.

As we began to set up our gear, Garth stopped me in my tracks. "Did you hear that?!" he whispered, staring down the hall. For an instant, I thought I heard someone running away, but I wasn't sure. Turning to him, I signaled walking with my fingers. He nodded in response. I collected myself before asking, "Is somebody up here?" of course there was nothing in response.

We decided to move on and head for the room I felt the strongest about. Something about it felt wrong, ominous even. That's where I always wanted to be. In the places where you can feel the fear building in your bones, thickening in your throat. We set up our camera, and I sat myself in the corner of the room ready to begin an Estes Session. If you are unaware of what the Estes Method is, it's very similar to playing a game of telephone except with Spirits in the mix.

In this session, I am blindfolded with an SB7 box in hand. Powered on at full volume, the sweeps are set to 100ms. All a spirit box is, is radio channels sweeping forward or backwards of your choosing. I prefer to set mine forward at the fastest setting, that way the sweeps don't have time to pick up words. All I want to hear is the white noise sweeping.

Taking the headphones, I announce 'I'm going under', and that's how we begin. Garth asks a series of questions pertaining to the location, hoping for a response. I didn't realize at the time; he also had the Ovilus 5 going.

The answers given during this session are quite confusing. Mind you, while I'm under the Estes Method, I cannot hear my Husband ask his questions, nor can I see him. It's important to desensitize yourself by blindfolding and the white noise. Otherwise, the experiment is pointless. It allows you to focus on nothing but the noise of the sweeps, repeating anything you may hear come through the device.

While under, I got a very eerie feeling something was drawing near. It started off subtle, like a prickle of electric energy filling the room. Traces of that energy licked at my left side. That's when I felt we weren't alone. Then an image flashed in my thoughts. An image of a starved man, skin and bone, huddling beside me. His body is pale and completely naked. But what stood out the most was his eyes. His eyes wide, pupils dilated, and completely fixated on me. I felt the need to announce this aloud to Garth. What I find intriguing about this moment is right after I tell Garth what I see, the Ovilus 5 says my name. Not my full name, mind you. My nickname.

Jess followed by Stare, Coincidence? Perhaps... I am unaware of this, but my mind is very aware of him. He felt he had a story to tell, needed to tell. He appeared desperate and broken. Lost in an abyssal void seeking anyone to hear his plea. As though his final moments had been washed away with time, but for him it was eternally looping. For that instant moment, there was recognition of his existence, and he knew it. He is one of the reasons I am always searching for answers.

After our session, we rejoined the others at the party. But I am still left with so many questions. Who was that man? What was he trying to tell me? Was he even real? More often than not we walk away from a place with more questions than answers. Whether you believe it or not, he felt as real as you and me. Regardless, I am always searching. I will never stop. What I do know is that Abyssal Lurker will be forever etched into my mind.

Jessica Marie Proctor

Taylor Payette

"What's on the on the 4th floor?"

With each step I took leading up to the entrance of The Rock Island Roadhouse, my center of gravity shifted – That's when I knew.

I paused on the top stair, holding firmly on to the steel railing, and thought, "Here we go."

Outside, the large, red-brick building emitted a foreboding energy, and walking through its doors felt like the beginning of a horror story brought to life. It was eerily quiet; the air was calm, but something else was happening just under the surface of my awareness that I couldn't explain.

The building's owner, Lisa Vinar, greeted me upon arrival, along with my two companions, paranormal investigators Kandi and Derek Slater (From the Ashes Paranormal Co-Founders). Lisa was kind and inviting. She carried herself with a softness that stood out amidst the undercurrent of buzzing and chaotic unseen activity.

Although I was new to paranormal investigation, I began to help the Slaters unload and set up their equipment. While they were well-practiced, having investigated this location several times before, I admitted that I had "absolutely no idea" what I was doing.

I would soon discover that, at The Rock Island Roadhouse, you don't need to know what you're doing to know that something hidden is in the room with you.

When Lisa first offered to begin a tour through the building, Derek declined to join us. Kandi explained, "Derek won't go up to the 4 th floor."

Derek Slater is a powerful medium, and I have witnessed his extreme sensitivity in different settings. Needless to say, when he refused to go up to the 4th floor, it piqued my curiosity.

"What's up on the 4th floor," I asked.

The group shared shocking, fascinating stories, so I decided I would attempt to boldly venture up there alone. Shortly following the group tour, I worked up some courage, took an ovilus (a tool investigators use that translates patterns in energy fields into specific words and phrases), and opened the door to head up the stairwell. I set my intentions on the 4th floor.

As soon as I began my journey into the unknown, the ovilus loudly emitted the word, "Murder!"

I jumped and abruptly shouted, "Oh my g-" before quickly returning to the 1st floor homebase. I asked the group, "Were they trying to scare me just now? Did they do that on purpose?" Lisa responded nonchalantly, "Yeah, they do that all the time." While she reassured me that it was just a "spirit prank," I asked myself three questions:

1. What if the spirits were expressing their true intentions?

2. What if the spirits on the first floor were warning me to avoid going up to the 4th floor alone?

3. What would have happened had I continued anyway?

After that experience, I dared not go anywhere above 2nd floor by myself. I silently pledged that I would only go up to the 4th floor with the group. What happened once I did shook me to my core.

4th Floor Room G5

"They like Taylor. She's just their type."

It was hot and humid at the top of the building. The 4th floor is lined with dozens of short steel doors leading into small rooms holding preserved remnants of the past. Wood and windows that seemed as old as the day the building was built gave each room a unique character. They all carried a distinct energy, and Lisa shared stories of different entities that occupied or frequently visited each. It would be the case that none of the rooms' energies were as distinct as that of room G5.

I remarked on a strong energetic presence before Lisa opened G5's door. I dipped my head down as we entered. We stood there quietly before Lisa mentioned, "I bet they like Taylor. She's just their type."

I silently panicked in the darkness, replying, "I don't know if that's a good thing or a bad thing."

We spent some time in the room before I became uncomfortable enough to ask to leave.

Lisa

shut the door behind Kandi and I and we carried on with normal conversation. With all our backs turned several feet away, G5's door cracked open with a loud SCREECH! I jumped and screamed, the hair on the back of my neck raising, and ran a few paces down the hall.

We had gone into many of the rooms on the 4 th floor, closing every door behind us, but the only door that opened behind our backs belonged to room G5 where Lisa said the spirits thought I was "just their type."

I highly recommend The Rock Island Roadhouse for investigators or individuals looking to make a true connection with the spirit realm. A rich history lies within its walls. Almost every room has its own story, but, if you do visit, you might want to go with a friend to prepare for the haunted 4 th floor.

Whatever you do, don't go up there alone.

From the Ashes Paranormal

Kathrine Sorilos

I had just arrived from Athens Greece and my first ever investigation in the USA was at the Haunted Rock Island Roadhouse in Rock Island, Illinois in 2022.

I am a Lead Investigator for the team From the Ashes Paranormal and very good friends with the Co-Founders of the team Kandi and Derek Slater.

One evening they held a paranormal event so there were a few guests taking part as well.

I was called by Kandi Slater to go down to the basement and have a little feel around the basement and conduct an investigation. In a little room in the basement there were a few guests standing around myself, Kandi and a couple of other investigators.

As soon as I walked in the room, I felt sadness, fear, loss dizziness I smelt blood as a psychic and also a Physical Trance Medium my clear senses were heightened. I saw a young woman skinny fragile with her hands tight up in a rope and blood trickling between her legs.

She looked at me and smiled so politely and said Hi, my name is Rose. I instantly jumped in a time loop back in time and her whole life span in front of me was like a short horror movie.

Let's not forget everyone leaves their residual imprint behind. She showed me how she was misused and lived in that little room in the basement tied up on the wall.

Raped tortured they hardly feed her or let her take a bath. She feels pregnant and from the constant raping she lost her baby while being tied up in that room.

I had the idea to reconstruct the whole event of her life so one of the guests offered to be tied up against the wall.

I sat across from our female guest, closed my eyes and tried to channel Rose. All of a sudden, the girl's voice changed from being loud and hearty to a very soft-spoken voice with hardly any life in it answering questions. I opened my eyes and suddenly looked at our guest and everyone was looking at her in shock. They even witnessed it on the CCTV upstairs.

Her whole face had morphed into another woman's face and all her features had changed! The girl to begin with her face was a little chubby and suddenly her cheeks and eyes became very hollow, and chin was more outwards.

It was Rose! I was channeling Rose!

All of a sudden, the girl came back to our reality and asked to be taken down because she felt tired and that something warm and sticky was trickling down her legs. We could all smell blood but there was no blood there. We actually witnessed Rose's miscarriage.

So, Kandi and I took the girl out of the ropes and took her upstairs and performed Reiki healing and protection. Made sure she was fine so we can move on as guests and our teammates come first in an investigation.

John Looney and Al Capone

After a while we went to the 4th floor together with Kandi Slater with a few guests and I asked each guest to stand individually in front of each door. With the doors from the rooms of the building open as a door represent gateways. When I did my rounds before investigating the 4th floor, I caught a glimpse of Johnnie aka John Looney.

With his dark blue suit his hat and holding a cane while limping.so I grabbed a cane from the ground floor that Lisa had handy and went up to start our investigation. We had everyone standing by the doorways, we were asking questions and were not getting many answers through the spirit boxes or any reactions from the rempods.

So, I decided to liven up things, grabbed the cane and started limping doing a representation of John

Looney walking up and down the hallway banging on the doors and telling his girls to get up because it was time to work.

I started speaking in Italian and Greek as we all know. Trying to provoke them slightly. In those days the biggest gangsters, especially in Chicago and Illinois, were run by the Greek and Italian mafia.

I called upon Al Capone to show himself as we all know Johnny and Al had a big fall out.

All of a sudden different rempods were going of at the same time. Through a spirit box and another guest that had necrophonics my name came through in a loud man's voice but not in English as in Kathrine but in Greek.

As in Katerina! I know because I am a Greek Aussie and it was says Shut up Katerina! Shut your mouth bitch! You bitch Katerina get out! F....off get out.

It was getting very aggravated through the spirit boxes as it swore nonstop and some guests were feeling a bit uneasy and some started getting aggravated and swearing back. So, Kandi and I decided to end that session.

We did some cleansing grounding and protection on our guests since we are both Reiki Master Healers. Channelling Helen the Madame of the Roadhouse

So, I decided to go up to the third floor. But this time I decided to go under the Estes Method.

First time ever. Being an Empath and a Sensitive as well any kind of spirit boxes do my head in. As a physical Trance Medium those devices and me don't see eye to eye! Let's not forget a Psychic / Medium is a device on their own.

So, I decided to dive into the Estes Method for the first time with only white noise. At the beginning I was answering some questions. I couldn't hear the questions, but I was answering.

After a while I stopped answering questions and I was telling a story. The story of the girls living there under the Tyrant Madam Helen and offering their services to different men.

Each one was standing behind locked doors whispering their sad story to me. Asking me to unlock their doors and set them free in tears to leave and see their families again

I was asking them who has the keys with tears streaming down my face I was speaking so loudly and crying and then suddenly I hear nothing but deafening silence.

I felt the presence of a chubby woman walking and stomping her feet like she was in the army. She was holding keys, a bunch of keys all hooked on a big round metal. Skeleton keys, old keys.

She was going around locking each door and telling each girl if they ever spoke again to anyone, they will never come out from that room again and if they do it will be feet first. (Dead)!

I could hear silent crying in my head. And then a deadly silence. I lasted only 20 minutes under the Estes Method. I thought I was under just a few minutes of a different timeline. Since then, I haven't done the Estes Method at another investigation, and it's been 2 years.

Kathrine Sorilos

Aaron G Thompson

Story told by Aaron G Thompson of Netflix's "28 Days Haunted."

In May 2018, I was invited to investigate a brand-new location—right in my neck of the woods! After hosting a sold-out ghost hunting event at a local haunted mansion, speaking at a paranormal-themed convention, and prepping for another late-night, team-only investigation with a renowned author, I received an invitation to experience the "Rock Island Haunted Roadhouse."

Exhausted as I was, the dedicated two-hour tour left such an impression that I've been coming back ever since.

The location was originally a YMCA, built in 1912, and is now a furniture store. I wanted to entice the unseen by setting up a sports-themed activity—a race.

Using two separate electromagnetic field detectors, each calibrated to different frequencies, I set up the race. I've never witnessed a more perfect five minutes of intelligent responses.

I boldly proclaimed, "I'm going to win because I have legs!" (I was feeling cheeky.) I explained the rules: to start the race, the spirit needed to hit one meter, then run to a mannequin at the end of the hallway and back. Upon returning, the spirit had to hit the other meter.

As I slouched over in the dark, making intense eye contact with the meters, one of them went off. I wasn't sure if it was real or just in my head. I looked around at everyone, and they all looked back at me, equally stunned. Then, as I rubbed my eyes and continued to focus, the meter lit up again.

I asked the crowd, "Are my eyes playing tricks on me, or did you all see that meter go off?" Everyone confirmed that they had seen it too.

Jokingly, I hiked up my pants and said, "Well, I better run now." A child named Madison, who was present, wanted to race with me, so she joined in.

After our jog back, I let Madison touch the meter first—rules are rules. The group informed me that the meter hadn't gone off. I joked, "It must have been a fat ghost."

Later, during post-review of the audio, we caught an Electronic Voice Phenomenon (EVP). When the meter went off the second time, and the race began, a voice clearly said, "Race me."

And after Madison and I completed the race, another EVP clearly stated, "Aaron won. No, Madison did." The unseen was correct—technically, I let her touch the finish line meter before me.

After I made the fat ghost joke, the second meter lit up brightly.

It's worth noting that the meters were in a room surrounded by stone walls and concrete floors—close enough to both meters that if something natural caused a spike, both would go off. After the meter lit up, the surveillance operator witnessed an anomaly on the cameras.

Was it just an orb or dust particle? We reviewed it on-site and saw a phenomenal crescent light that held a static position, moved, then faded on camera. The dust particles were high in the camera frame, moving upward, and looked vastly different.

I quickly took the crew back into the room for a spirit box session to confirm—once again—who won the race.

Drum roll, please...

"Madison." The name came through loud and clear.

All of this happened within five minutes. It was recorded on two cameras and one external audio device. This is what researchers seek—solid evidence, documented.

The Rock Island Haunted Roadhouse chose me that day.

Aaron G Thompson & Kat Grace

Kat Grace

Story told by Kat Grace.

I was recently told about my person, Aaron, experiencing seeing shadows, or shadow people for the first time—a form of ghostly apparition presentation per observer.

I never expected what happened next.

Lisa, the owner, was kind enough to allow us some research time on location in November of 2023—just us two in the HUGE furniture warehouse of The Rock Island Haunted Roadhouse.

With dusk turning black and our gear buzzed and ready to roll, I was anxious to join Aaron in the basement, where he'd been having very unique scenarios happen... This is definitely one of my tops.

We seated ourselves in the darkness of the basement, tucked in a back room with only the hum of the lights on what devices we had present, nearing a door.

The door which caused a reaction with Aaron to witness a first...

Not expecting to receive a similar experience, I was amped up to hear what type of conversation we'd engage via our spirit box.

With the noise rolling—intelligent conversation from the unseen and us engaging—in the wiggle of darkness, a warped visional forefront of mine. I began to see transparent, almost pure 3D-style shadows moving about.

Aaron allowed me to take in the phenomenon. As I exclaimed, "I'm seeing shadow people," we both started confirming at the same time the movements and locations of the ghosts.

It was truly a wild experience, and for that—this location has my heart.

From the Ashes Paranormal

My Friend.....Mr. Looney By Derek Slater

From the Ashes Paranormal Hello, let me introduce myself. My name is Derek Slater, co-founder of From the Ashes Paranormal. From the time I was 12 years old, I knew I wasn't like other kids. I could see and hear things, others couldn't. It wasn't until I watched "Paranormal Kids," that I understood my differences were actually a gift.

A gift, that at times becomes a burden. I am not only an empath, but a physical and trance medium. I can see and hear the dead and allow them to speak through me.

I first came to the Haunted Rock Island Roadhouse in 2018, when it was known as the Haunted YMCA, Rock Island. I'll never forget my first visit. As I approached the building for the first time, I knew it was definitely more than just a YMCA, I knew there was a deeper darker history. I couldn't wait to go in and finally embrace my gifts. For many years, I pushed my gifts back, and refused to let them show, causing me to fall into a deep depression.

No, more, this would be the first time I truly embraced my gifts with others. When Lisa, the owner of the building, who has become a mother figure to me gave me a tour of the building, we first made our way into the basement. It was in the boiler room, where I first met the notorious madam Helen Van Dale for the first time. She was a very prim and proper woman. She was there visiting the janitor, whom it was clear she had a thing for. She looked me up and down, turned her nose up to me and went about her business, discussing her "resorts." Resorts are what brothels were called during her era.

As we made our way from the boiler room to the boy's locker room, it was there that I encountered a woman who seemed to be out of place. A woman foaming from the mouth. It appeared she had an encounter with some type of poison. Just recently I found out why I was seeing her. She lived in one of the houses on the property before it became a YMCA. She had ingested a poison, resulting in her death.

Upon returning to the main floor, Lisa pointed out where the dining room, and gymnasium were. I kept seeing a happy young man dressed as a clown, running around holding a bright red balloon. All I could do was smile and give him a pleasant nod, saying hello. I couldn't quite figure out why I was seeing a clown. Turns out the YMCA held a yearly circus in their gymnasium.

As we made our way upstairs to the second floor, I felt an overwhelming sense of sadness as we approached what Lisa would identify as the trunk room. Here I would see women huddled close to the ground, beaten and crying. I also felt as though a woman, or women were beaten to the point of miscarriage. I felt a lump in my throat and my eyes began to swell. "I need to get out of this room," I said.

As we slowly walked down the dark hallways of the second and third floors, I would see many spirits who wanted to visit with me, all eager to tell their stories. I felt they were happy to have another visitor who could see and hear them.

Then it was time, time to visit the 4th floor. As we slowly walked up the stairs, the closer we got to the fourth floor, the more the hair on the back of my neck stood up. As we reached the top of the floor, I knew without a doubt there was a lot of upset energies on this floor. I was immediately drawn to the right.

As Lisa led us down the long hallway, it was so quiet, you could hear a pin drop. We stopped at a doorway labeled G5. I took a deep breath, as Lisa slowly opened the door. As I breached the doorway, I'll never forget what I saw. A middle-aged man from the 1920's, wearing nothing but a pair of pants, curled up in the back left corner of the room. He appeared to be severely beaten. "Please don't, I promise I'll keep my mouth shut. I'll never speak of what I saw again." he said terrified. I looked at him and, in my mind, assured him I was not there to hurt him. I would later learn that he was beaten within inches of his life in this room. He would then be dragged out of the room by a man name Bob, who would throw him down the elevator shaft to his death.

As we left room G5, we turned right and headed down the long hallway, which was glowing red from the exit light. As we walked down the hallway I would see a silhouette of a slender man, with a top hat and cane near the end of the hall. It was none other than Mr. John Looney, the infamous mobster whom it is said that Al Capone himself feared.

As we continued down the hallway, I began to see his facial features. He had a stone face and glared at me as he took a few steps towards me limping and using his cane to hold him up. He began mumbling about how this was his building, and I better do as he said. He came at me as if we were playing a game of cat and mouse, testing me to see just how much I could see and hear. I knew without a doubt he was someone people did not want to mess with.

On several future visits to the Roadhouse, I continued to play this game of cat and mouse with Mr. Looney. We have had many sessions where I have spoken to Mr. Looney, (note I call him Mr. Looney out of respect.). Mr. Looney takes a liking to mediums as I would come to learn. He was always very intimidating. He would even jump into me from time to time. By jump into me I am referring to something like the movie Ghost. There is a point in the movie where Whoopie Goldberg's character Ida Mae allows Patrick Swayze's character Sam to enter her to communicate with Molly, Demi Moore's character.

Once Sam leaves Oda Mae, she is completely drained of energy. This is very similar to what would happen when Mr. Looney would jump into me.

I'll never forget the time I was standing at the T intersection of the 4th floor hallway adjacent to Mr. Looney's room with my wife Kandi, Lisa, and our friend Stacey. Kandi indicated that Mr. Looney was communicating with her on some equipment in his room. I remember looking up at the red exit light and seeing Mr. Looney limping towards me. Then boom he was in me. The next thing I remember, Lisa was walking me down the hall. "What are we doing here?" I asked Lisa. "He was in you again." Lisa said. The second I came back to the rempod in Mr. Looneys room went off, indicating he was now back in his room. Lisa and Kandi were quick to get me down to the first floor. They both could not believe what they had just witnessed. They both were discussing the way I glared at Kandi and how my face was literally transforming in front of their eyes. They both at the same time pointed to a photo of Mr. Looney and said, "This is what I saw." From then on, I had a love, hate relationship with him.

My relationship with Mr. Looney recently changed. During the summer of 2024, I was on the 3rd floor painting the new doll room. Mr. Looney would venture down to the 3rd floor and periodically peek in on me. He was very curious as to what I was doing. I was shocked when one day, nearing the end of my painting with his cold stare he gave me a nod and said, "thank you," turned around and left. It appeared he was recognizing that I was improving "his" home. I feel our relationship reached new levels when Lisa and Kandi were on a conference call with Lili of Haunted Happy Hour, Inc.

They were discussing a new, custom blend of coffee that would be made exclusively for the Roadhouse and be featured at the 2nd Annual Haunted Rock Island Roadhouse Paracon. As the ladies were discussing different coffee flavor options, "I have some input," I interrupted. All three of the ladies were shocked to hear me talk, as I'm normally very quiet. They were all ears. "Helen is here," I said, "she would like a coffee with hints of cherry and something sweet." Then to my surprise Mr. Looney came forward. He indicated he would like something earthy, maybe hints of whiskey or cinnamon, yes cinnamon. I quickly relayed his preferences as well.

Again, he thanked me and quickly went about his business. Lisa, Kandi and Lili were all excited. Lili would take the suggestions back to the rest of the Haunted Happy Hour team and get back with their creations. Ultimately, the flavor would be based off Helen's preferences. Helen's Black Forest Blend was officially born. Since that day, Mr. Looney has shown me a newfound respect.

I still don't like to enter his territory of the 4th floor but when I am at the Roadhouse and he is on the main floor, he kindly nods to say hello as he goes about his business. Almost as if we are, dare I say it, friends.

Derek Slater

S & S Paranormal Investigations

Founder: Tony Salazar Jr.

This happened on my very 1st time there. We were in the Trunk Room. 2nd Floor. We were during a Til Midnight investigation.

Linda the medium was conducting a EVP session with our group, telling us about the room and its history. During the session, my friend Minda became very emotional and left the room weeping. Everyone became concerned and puzzled about Minda.

Since the 2nd floor is associated w women of the night, and to lighten the mood of the room, I announced to the female spirits that I was single, I have a job, a pocket full of cash and I'm looking for a date.

Everyone laughed and Linda continued the EVP session. As Linda was talking, I felt my left arm, by my shoulder being squeezed. I look to my left and there is a woman named Nicki sitting crossed legged on the floor. She feels me staring her way because the room is dark and asks me 'what?" I asked if she touched me, and she replied "No! And why would I touch you!" So at that point I asked Linda the medium to look in my direction. She looks and says "yeah, there's a woman standing to the left of you, why?" I replied I had felt my left arm being squeezed. She replied smiling, " well you were wanting a date!" Ha ha ha! 😁

Tony Salazar Jr.

Quad Cities Spirit Realm Investigators

By Amanda Thomas

Haunted YMCA, R.I. experience - One of the experiences I had at the Old YMCA, now the Haunted Rock Island Roadhouse that was memorable to me, was on the 4th floor.

I was with a group of people, and we had just finished a couple EVP sessions; (Electronic Voice Phenomenon; this is where you capture voices or sounds on a recorder), and we were asking questions that we were getting responses to on our devices.

We were leaving one side of the building and walking down the hallway to the stairs when a guy behind me yelled and then dropped down to the floor. As this happened, I was in front of him and suddenly had a very painful pinch on my behind. I turned around, and the guy was unresponsive to what we were saying to him, so everyone helped him get up and down the stairs where he eventually snapped out of it and said all he remembered was being rushed up on by something.

Someone else said they saw a black shadow go by fast like it was running. I said that must have been something that pinched me. It hurt for a good hour afterward. I never had that happen before. It was almost like being stung by a bee. This was of course, one of my most memorable experiences in this building, although I've had many more.

Amanda Thomas
QCSRI

Justin Cardamone

QCSRI

Silent Explorers

By Josey Roberts

March 2021 The Silent Explorers team (Jason, Michael, and Josey) have been together for six years and we have investigated many locations.

In March 2021, we attended the Rock Island Haunted YMCA event and conducted a paranormal investigation on the fourth floor.

After we investigated one room at the end of the hall, we decided to walk down the long hall. Jason and Mike were behind me (Josey) and I was holding the video camera with an infrared light.

We walked slowly because the hallway was so dark, we could only see through the video camera screen.

Suddenly, I stopped and saw what looked like a very black hand and arm reach out of the door on the left and it tried to hit my face. I jumped back quickly but felt a very cold touch on my left cheek. I looked around but saw nothing. I felt a cold spot around me and felt sick to my stomach. I told Mike to go in front and I moved to the middle, with Jason behind me.

We continued walking down the hall. Mike walked near the emergency door area. I felt something was wrong, so I turned back to look at Jason, He was just standing there frozen, staring at something on the other side of the hall. Suddenly, he began to be frightened and started running. He kept looking back and running again.

I felt very cold air surround us as we ran after him. I grabbed Jason and held him to calm down, but he kept looking at the floor like something was crawling towards him. Finally, he calmed down and said he saw a dark black shadow come at him. He felt it was going to attack him, so he ran away from it. I've known Jason for a long time, and I never saw him so frightened before. We never forgot about that night. It was one of the most dramatic paranormal investigations in Silent Explorers history.

Josey Roberts

Alisha Friedericks

The men's ward is where I've gotten the most activity, to me it always seemed that they were uncomfortable with women being in their area.

Most memorable and active night for me there, another female colleague and I spent time in that area, we were seeing tall shadows crossing the hall back and forth from different rooms. A lot of banging, we stood at the end of the hall near the stairwell so as not to disrespect anyone or invade their space.

We got a lot of interaction with the rem pod when asking questions if it was ok that we were there talking to them, they responded with no. They didn't like us being in their space but still interacted with us.

Eventually they would answer other questions we were asking if they enjoyed it there and if the building was their home, to which they replied with yes. That night was the most interaction we had, the gentleman on the floor weren't too fond of us being there but still interacted to let us know lol the shadows we were seeing were tall and broad shoulder, they didn't come down our way but were crossing the hall going from room to room or peering out behind the doors. It was an interesting night for sure!

Quad Cities Spirit Realm Investigators

By Justin Cardamone

One of my most memorable experiences at the Old YMCA, now known as the Haunted Rock Island Roadhouse, is when several investigators were on the 4th floor in a long, dark hallway and had a spirit box going.

We were getting several intelligent responses to our questions, and some responses were even beyond the scope of what we were asking.

As we all took turns asking questions and interacting, one investigator opened himself up to the spirits. As some of us surrounded him in case we were needed, he became silent and in tune with them. After only a few minutes, he went from standing to completely collapsing and myself and a couple others jumped in to catch him. He was not fully oriented or able to walk on his own. We got him down to the first floor and in a chair as he slowly came out of it.

Thankfully he ended up being just fine, and we held off investigating up there for a while. This is, by far, one of my most memorable experiences at an amazing location!

Dez Darling Vine

It's difficult to single out just one experience in Vinar, given how active the place is.

It's where I first saw shadowy figures peering out from doorways, had doors slamming shut on their own, and encountered mysterious phantom smells.

But my most unforgettable moment took place on the 4th floor. As I was recounting the building's mob-connected history to my husband, I mentioned John Looney's name. Instantly, I felt the presence of two figures standing shoulder to shoulder with me, despite my husband being three doors down at the time.

I voiced what I was experiencing out loud, only to have my hair tugged—my first physical encounter with a spirit. That day, I learned the importance of protecting myself from otherworldly energies.

Dez Darling Vine

Lisa Vinar

A lot of people ask why I would want to own a haunted old YMCA, and why they should investigate my building.

They say, it's a YMCA, people enjoyed coming to my building. It was a happy place. I smile and say, there's a lot more to it than you think. A lot of things happened in my building that were kept secret......everything was a secret.

Let me start at the beginning and explain that when this all started, I was a big chicken. I was unfamiliar with this since my past experiences were so many years ago.

So, the first couple of times it really scared me. It had been years since living in my mother's house and witnessing my father haunting the house watching over his family. He passed away at the age of 38, and left a wife and 6 children behind, so I believe this is why he stayed behind.

This is why I also believe Dan; my late husband is still here. He kept saying while he was in the hospital that he had to get back to the store, hence my first couple of encounters I believe were with him making sure his business was in order.

My first experience in my building happened after closing. I had closed and locked the door and went into the bathroom in my office. I started hearing sounds like someone was in my office moving around and shuffling papers. I called out, "Who's there?" but no one answered. This went on a few times with no answer. Finally, I reached out, grabbed my phone and called my son. I had him stay on the line with me until I got my things and out of the building.

The second experience was when one of my other boys bought me my recorder. I decided to try it out as I swept in the main stairwell. I set it at the edge of the 3rd floor landing while I swept. When I finished sweeping, I came down and listened to it. I was shocked by what I heard. It was my mother's voice. My mother was saying my name, calling out to me. Again, I got out of the building right away.

I gained some courage after this and was somewhat used to the spirits. Again, after closing, I put my recorder behind my desk on my computer and said, "there you go Dan, talk to me." I went into the bathroom, as this seems to be a hot spot for spirits to bug me when I go in there. I was in there a little while, when I heard the door by my office slam. I called out, "What was that." And heard nothing. Again, I listened to my recording and immediately heard shuffling and someone moving around as if they were going through things.

After the door slam, I heard my voice, followed by heavy breathing on my recorder. I found this strange and asked a couple of investigators how this was possible.

It was explained to me that some spirits don't realize they have passed away and so they continue to breathe. I didn't run this time.

One of the most interesting stories is when we were having a public investigation. One young man didn't believe in spirts and was mocking them, being disrespectful.

We had told people not to go into one of the rooms upstairs because Derek had been attacked there earlier. Instead of paying attention to this warning, when we were on free roam, this young man decided to go up there by himself. The next thing I heard was that there was a guest crying out in the parking lot and refused to come back inside. It was that young man.

Apparently when he went into the room, he said all he could remember was his life flashing before his eyes and waking up on the floor. Needless to say, he is now a believer. I have many, many more stories and experiences, but you should come enjoy your own experiences.

Dr. Rebecca Foster

Things That Make You Go, Hmm.

I am Dr Rebecca Foster, clairvoyant medium. I have been practicing for 38 years but gifted my entire life. I can see, hear, and speak to those passed over, including animals both living and passed, and non-verbal energies who are living. I am a medical intuitive, remote viewer, author, and public speaker.

My life has been dedicated to serving Yahweh in any capacity He feels I should be, and His will rules my world. I believe this background is needed to understand who I am and what makes up my abilities and purpose. I believe that those nearest to Yahweh's desires in one's life are the most tormented, to deter their paths.

I was invited by a friend to the Roadhouse to do a private, overnight investigation. Having never been there before, I was terribly excited, especially not knowing anything about it. I arrived during the day and met the owner Lisa, who said she never stays after dark. This struck me as even more exciting, because the owner, who should be comfortable with her establishment, won't stay into the night.

My friend, Allen, had been to the Roadhouse many times, was a big man, had shamanic energy, practiced healing flute and Native music, and made me feel like I could be safe working. What I mean is that, when I open myself up to speak to these energies, they can affect my energy, my abilities, and may attack, so I need someone around me who can help me get out if needed.

Allen and I did a quick walk through in the light so I could catch my bearings. We started off in the basement section. A long hallway under a ramp, full of storage units. This area was once the pool, but was backfilled due to several reasons, including the drowning of a young man.

We walked into the dark halls full of doors, some open, some locked and I could feel eyes upon me. Now keep in mind, in the dark, for me, it is just as hard to see some of these energies as anyone unless they present in a lighted way. As we were leaving the hallway, Allen said, "Open this door and check this out." I opened an unlocked door on the left and walked into the entry. As my eyes focused, I could see a chair in the middle of the room with mirrors all around it. I jumped out and yelled, 'No way!! Why would you let me go in this room!" It was a scrying room and very dangerous when used improperly. Mirrors can be used to open portals and when reflecting each other, create an unknown pathway for demonic and negative energies to enter buildings and locations.

I was not happy, not angry, more so very strongly opinionated about even being in that presence. I immediately told Lisa how bad it was and that anyone doing that there could ruin the good energy at the property. I've seen it happen.

Allen and I walked the remaining portions of the building in the light, but that basement section never left my thoughts. I knew that was where I would meet the darkness in the building later in the night.

I encountered several human energies on upper levels, some of whom were quite talkative and not menacing. I was excited to get investigating this old building due to the history during the 1920s. For this, I brought a small bottle of alcohol to entice those who I knew would have stayed in this location while traveling.

The meat of the night. Oh my gosh, it was amazing. I will say now that the Roadhouse is one of the topmost haunted locations I have ever visited. I mean the top three most haunted next to Ashmore Estates and the Cheney Mansion.

Allen and I were on the second level in the classroom area. We set up cameras pointing to the doorway where earlier and man named Ryan spoke to me, words that were caught on camera. We put electromagnetic field (EMF) detectors and towers in the hallway leading from where Ryan was to the room we were in. I opened the alcohol bottle, set it on the table and yelled, "Alcohol!!! It's yours, all you must do is come and get it!" Allen placed a device against the bottle that when moved, it screamed in alarm.

Allen and I sat at a table and went live on social media. I proceeded to read people in the online chat room to increase the energy in the building. We continued to talk about the delicious alcohol on the table and converse with people online. Suddenly, I saw Ryan's shadow, and you could see the detectors lighting up as Ryan came down the hallway, and then the alarm went off, screaming as someone attempted to take the bottle. The lights went back off in the opposite direction, and Ryan was gone.

We assured him that the alarm would not hurt him, and it happened a second time, but that was it. He didn't come back a third time. We finished the online event, cleaned up and left that bottle as a reward for Ryan.

We moved to the main floor, mattress section. Allen said there was a prostitute's energy in the back section who would touch men who laid on the bed. So, we tested that theory with Allen lying on the bed and me on another. He placed a $20 bill on the bed and after no touches, we started talking about moving. We continued an electronic voice phenomenon (EVP) session and suddenly, we heard thumping loud walking on the other side of the wall. The ramp to the basement was on the other side of the wall and not only was I excited to go see what it was, I was a little worried. Let me back up here.

When Lisa, the owner locked up, she set an alarm on the back door. Earlier in the evening, Allen and I had ordered food and when the delivery person showed up, an alarm went off when the doorway was opened. This comforted me to know that if someone tried to get into the building, we would hear the door open.

Fast forward to us in the mattress room. We hear the noise on the other side of the wall and high tail it to the doorway leading into the ramp and loading dock. I walked onto the ramp, lights on at this point for us and nothing there. Allen walked to the door to join me and the door alarm went off. We looked at each other like who is here?? Allen said he would go check the door and be right back. I said, "okay" and waited in the ramp area. I then realized that the energy in the basement from earlier, was trying to separate Allen and I and moved to join him by the front door.

I explained what had just happened and told him I would not go into the basement alone due to this attempt to get me alone. At this point we needed to see who was in the basement, so we set up cameras on the ramp leading to the basement storage area. As we were investigating, I heard, "Come here." I knew it was not human, more enticing and creepier. I am not one to call in elephants nor play with things that can hurt me. It was asking me to come to the bottom of the ramp. In that moment, a man dressed in jeans and a blue top, with brown curly hair came around the corner from the basement and stood at the bottom of the ramp. He had zero eyes, more like black circles. NOT human. He asked me to join him. No way in hell was I going down there with him. Allen said, "I'll go," and I was worried for him, asking him if he really wanted to do that.

Allen walked down the ramp to the point where it turned into the basement and stood there. He stood for a minute saying there was nothing and then without warning or a word, Allen said something incoherent and came running up the ramp. He ran past me and into a room where we were storing all our equipment. He waved to me to remove the camera off him and stood to catch his breath.

He seemed rattled and out of sorts. It took him a few minutes, but later said that something, a dark mass, came out of one of the hallways and moved towards him. I knew we needed to investigate this more, but at that point, it was outsmarting us, and we took a break from the ramp/loading dock area.

We ended the night with many more questions than when we started. We met several interesting energies who were simply sticking around, not just residual energies, but those choosing to stay. I even made friends with the 'house' ghost who ran the 4th floor. We slept on the couches in the front of the building and surprisingly, everything left us alone.

In the morning, in the bright sunlight, the building seemed less foreboding. I told Allen I was going to get my equipment gathered and packed up and put in my car. Allen explained that we had to leave through the basement after locking the doors. I was like, "Wait....

what? We must go in the basement???" I asked myself quietly if Allen was able to do this himself, but realistically could not let him go down there alone after what we had experienced. We proceeded to get our things to leave. I went to the room where our equipment was stored, gathered up all I could carry and went outside with my load. I came back inside and could not find Allen. I stood in the equipment room and yelled, "Allen! Allen, where are you!? Allen????"

I walked out into the ramp area and saw the lights were on in the basement. I heard movement and thought, "Allen must be doing his Shamanic flute down there to clear the energy." I didn't put this past him. I yelled, "Allen, what are you doing? Okay, I'm coming to join you." I walked down the ramp, into the basement as far as the hallway took me, right to the side hall with the scrying mirror. I was standing under the ramp near the old pool and yelled, "Allen, where are you!?" Allen replied, "I'm here!" "Where I replied." "Up here?" "Up where!!??" He replied, "I'm up here!" It hit me at that moment that I was lured to the basement. Made to think Allen was downstairs and he absolutely was not. I turned and ran as fast as I could. I laughed a bit at how smart that demonic energy was in convincing me I was safe. How stupid could I be?? But it was that convincing.

We went on about that for a while, just not believing what had just happened. It was an awesome ending to the investigation. We got the rest together and went to the basement to leave. Allen had keys that were needed to unlock the door from the inside and lock it from the outside again. We went down the dark stairs into the darker basement where I knew the really bad things had remained. We went through a mechanics room and a dim light appeared from a small window near the doorway.

Allen proceeded to the door, and I watched our back. Imagine the scene in Titanic when the water is rising, and Jack and Rose are trying to get the keys to unlock that gate from the wrong side.... This is the only way to explain how desperate I was for him to unlock that door. He fumbled in the dark to insert the key and from behind us, he approached. I literally said, "Allen.... did you get it yet?" He replied that it was a bit tricky. As that menacing energy neared, Allen unlocked the door, and it opened from a very stuck position. I raced past him and pulled the door shut. Whew! I never wanted to do that again.

I was so relieved to be out of there. I also felt like I never needed to investigate there again. I lied to myself at that moment. That investigation made me want to find out more.

I put together another investigation with a team and a full live recording of everything we did. My son Bradley joined me along with my good friend Rob Klaus, who has sadly since passed away. Rob and I had an amazing connection when investigating and I trusted him in every way to keep me safe. Long story short, Rob went into the basement, alone to do an Estes Method session. This is when the senses are blocked and the only thing heard is from a radio sweep, which energy is used to produce words and sentences. The person is blindfolded, and noise cancelling headphones are placed over the ears.

Our purpose was to prove that the Estes method was a real phenomenon and that I was a real medium. I went upstairs with the rest of the crew and watched on camera as Rob sat alone in a pitch-black basement. I watched as a man entered behind Rob and I felt a chill up my back, which I commented on. Rob said, "I'm on your back." I asked the guy if he was in the building. I then said, you drowned in the pool. Then Rob said, "Drowning."

The tech guy and I both dropped our mouths open to the responses. This conversation went on for about 10 minutes when Rob said he was done. Bradley and another crew member ran down to him to make sure he was safe. The whole conversation was caught live on camera as thousands watched. There was no way either of us could hear the other, and it proved that these tools, including me, were genuine. Our evening produced much evidence of the afterlife, and we all left quite happy with what was revealed.

I'll finish by saying that the Roadhouse is not only historical, it is alive. I would say to any future investigators to enter with full respect and knowledge of what you're planning on doing while you're there. Respect the property and lifelong residents. You do not need to conjure or invoke anything else into the building, as there is enough there already. Thank you for reading my story.

By Dr Rebecca Foster

Katie Thompson

My first time investigating the Rock Island Roadhouse, I was invited by my friend Kandi. My partner, Kalina, and I drove down from Wisconsin and the trip was well worth the drive.

My most memorable experience happened on the fourth floor. A group was investigating one of the hallways with a spirit box before we got there and was getting many seemingly intelligent direct responses. Once they left, Kalina and I set up a myriad number of trigger and sensor items: cat balls, REM Pods, motion sensor music boxes, a couple of cameras, etc.

We had heard the story of the noise in the elevator shaft on the other side of the building, so Kalina went to put a digital recorder by the elevator while I stayed in the hallway and started an EVP session. Once Kalina's footsteps had faded, it was very quiet, and I turned on my recorder.

I sat in a room off the hall (because it already had a chair) and started asking questions. I was still very quiet. After a few moments of silence and the questions, a music box at the dead end of the hall sounded. The noise was startling in the dark and silent hallway. I called for Kalina but got no response. I stayed put and continued my EVP session and the music box chimed again. I stepped out into the hall to investigate and that is when Kalina returned, from the open end of the hall, opposite the music box and too far away to trigger the sensor.

I let her know what had been happening and we immediately tried to find out what had tripped the sensor. There was no evidence of animals or rodents, it wasn't pointed at a door or window that could move or cast shadow, and no one else was up there.
We checked and replaced the batteries.

I walked around until I found the edges of the sensor field; there was nothing within that space that should have triggered the motion sensor. I was stumped.

We sat in the hallway for a while, asking questions and we had a cat ball in one of the rooms that blinked frequently, seeming to respond at times. After about an hour of nothing and no one, the music box sang out again. Once again, we investigated. Nothing. It happened 3 more times that evening. We had two other investigators come up and inspect the set-up and we could not find the source.

To this day, I have no idea what was moving in that room to trigger the music box.

Chapter 7

Photo Gallery

This is what remains of the original spiral staircase in the building when it was a YMCA

Photo courtesy of Kandi Slater

Front Door

Photo courtesy of Michael Jonathan

Gymnasium

Photo courtesy of Kandi Slater

Boiler Room with original boilers

Photo courtesy of Kandi Slater

New doll room on the 3rd floor. Opened in 2024.

Photo Courtesy of Kandi Slater

Front of building

Photo courtesy of Michael Jonathan

The floor in what used to be the gymnasium. You can still see some of the gym floor markings.

Photo courtesy of Kandi Slater

Blueprint of the entrance

Photo courtesy of Lisa Vinar

Old Wrestling Room. This is where a spirit we call Rose spends a lot of time. As this is where she was chained to the wall.

Photo courtesy of Kandi Slater

What was the Boys Locker Room

Photo courtesy of Kandi Slater

Hallway in what used to be the pool. At the end of the hall is a portal. Photo taken standing where the diving board was in the deep end looking at shallow end.

Photo courtesy of Kandi Slater

This is the running track still in the building from when it was an ymca. The track overlooks the gymnasium.

Photo courtesy of Michael Jonathan

Cornerstone, there's a time capsule behind it.

Photo courtesy of Kandi Slater

Elevator shaft at the top of 4th floor.

Photo courtesy of Kandi Slater

One of the many hallways.

Photo courtesy of Kandi Slater

This is written in the infamous trunk room.

Photo courtesy of Lisa Vinar

Final Thoughts

As you close the final chapter of "Whispers in the Walls: Ghosts of the Rock Island Roadhouse," the echoes of history and legend resonate deeply. This book has taken you beyond the surface of a seemingly ordinary building, revealing the dark and fascinating past that has shaped its very essence. The Rock Island Roadhouse is not just a structure of brick and mortar; it is a keeper of secrets, a witness to the notorious figures who once walked its halls.

Al Capone and John Looney, names synonymous with crime and power, left their indelible marks on this place. Their presence, along with the whispers of countless others, continues to haunt the walls of the Roadhouse, creating an atmosphere thick with tension and intrigue. Through this exploration, you've delved into the lives of those who thrived in the shadows, who built empires on fear, and who left behind a legacy that refuses to fade.

This book is more than a collection of ghost stories; it's a chronicle of a bygone era, a time when lawlessness and the supernatural intertwined in a dance of danger and mystery. The Rock Island Roadhouse stands as a monument to that time, its walls still reverberating with the energy of those who once called it home—both in life and in death. As you reflect on the tales within these pages, remember that some stories never truly end; they continue to linger, whispering through the walls, waiting to be discovered once more.

ABOUT THE AUTHOR

 Scott E. Bowser is the author of three non-fiction books, Gein (2021), The Travelers Guide to Ed Gein (2021) and The Ed Gein Chronicles (2023). Scott appeared on MGM Plus tv show "Psyco: The Lost Tapes of Ed Gein" and Wisconsin Ghostly Legends (2024)

Scott was born in 1964, in Kingsford, Michigan and lived his young years in Neenah, Wisconsin. Scott always had an interest in true crime and the paranormal whether it be reading about it or watching it on tv.

Scott now lives in Wisconsin Rapids. Wisconsin where in his spare time he gives Ed Gein tours in Plainfield, Wisconsin. Scott also in his spare time creates children and adult coloring books which all are also available on Amazon. He is currently writing a screenplay for his first book "Gein".

Other Books by Scott Bowser

Available on Amazon

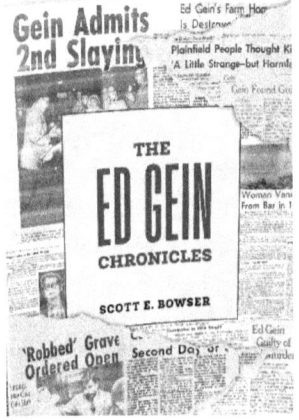

www.ingramcontent.com/pod-product-compliance
Lightning Source LLC
LaVergne TN
LVHW012020060526
838201LV00061B/4390